Praise for

BE THE CALM
OR BE THE STORM

I have been fortunate to have competed against and worked with some very strong women, all with unique traits that have made them leaders in their respective fields. What stands out the most about Captain Sandy is that she is a true leader. One who leads with wisdom through experience—the wisdom to be passionate and compassionate, graceful yet strong, all while serving the ever-present roles of captain and mentor. As an author, Captain Sandy offers tools and tips on how to take control of one's life and how doing so gives us the best chance of excelling at whatever we choose. In this compelling and engaging narrative, she proves that anyone is capable of navigating the storms of life.

— **Gigi Fernández**, professional tennis player and Olympic gold medalist

Captain Sandy is effectively the CEO of the vessel she captains, leading with calm, confidence, and humanity. For those looking to lead in any industry, or even to govern themselves, readers will be inspired by the unique and skillful way she navigates the stormiest of seas.

— **Lisa Lutoff-Perlo**, president and CEO of Celebrity Cruises

I have known this woman since she was scrubbing barnacles off the bottom of boats. Captain Sandy brings a positive and contagious energy to everything she does, including the breathtaking storytelling she has gifted us through this book. It not only inspires readers with wisdom to help them chart their own course, it entertains, just like Captain Sandy herself.

— **John Flynn**, CEO of Fleet Advantage

Captain Sandy is a woman who has earned every stripe, standing tall at the helm of the superyachts she steers. What is most astonishing about her story is not just the calm and focused way she leads through crisis (which I was firsthand witness to when she faced pirates on the Red Sea), but the way she triumphed over her past and has remained committed to sobriety for more than three decades.

— **John Allen**, CEO of Quantum Marine Stabilizers

Sandy Yawn is not only a terrific captain, she is a shrewd and enterprising businesswoman, all of which I personally witnessed during her time at the helm. Whether you want to start a business, lead a company, or be a yacht captain yourself, these chapters are packed with wise words and examples to launch your own success.

— **James H. Herbert II**, founder and executive chairman
of First Republic Bank

This is a leadership book that is as unique as Captain Sandy's approach and life experience. She gets to the heart of what it means to be a servant leader—someone who puts the greater good above herself, whether that is taking care of charter guests, developing the skill sets of her crew, or assuring the safety of all souls on board. From harrowing tales of 20-foot seas to comic episodes with demanding and eccentric guests, these pages contain leadership lessons for anyone from a student of the navigation industry to a Fortune 500 executive.

— **Romaine Seguin**, CEO of Good360, former president of
UPS Global Freight Forwarding

Captain Sandy's fascinating stories about her experience at the helm of megayachts translate equally well into the C-suite and boardrooms of the business world. The lessons captured in her stories and captain's log can help leaders of every stage and situation navigate the changing and unpredictable waters of today's corporate world. As an educator of entrepreneurial leadership, I think this should be required reading for every current and aspiring entrepreneur.

— **Rebecca J. White, Ph.D.**, Walter Distinguished Chair of
Entrepreneurship, director of the John P. Lowth
Entrepreneurship Center, University of Tampa

BE THE CALM
OR BE THE STORM

BE THE CALM
OR BE THE STORM

Leadership Lessons from a Woman at the Helm

Captain Sandy Yawn

with SAMANTHA MARSHALL

HAY HOUSE

Carlsbad, California • New York City
London • Sydney • New Delhi

Published in the United Kingdom by:
Hay House UK Ltd, The Sixth Floor, Watson House,
54 Baker Street, London W1U 7BU
Tel: +44 (0)20 3927 7290; Fax: +44 (0)20 3927 7291; www.hayhouse.co.uk

Published in the United States of America by:
Hay House Inc., PO Box 5100, Carlsbad, CA 92018-5100
Tel: (1) 760 431 7695 or (800) 654 5126
Fax: (1) 760 431 6948 or (800) 650 5115; www.hayhouse.com

Published in Australia by:
Hay House Australia Ltd, 18/36 Ralph St, Alexandria NSW 2015
Tel: (61) 2 9669 4299; Fax: (61) 2 9669 4144; www.hayhouse.com.au

Published in India by:
Hay House Publishers India, Muskaan Complex, Plot No.3, B-2,
Vasant Kunj, New Delhi 110 070
Tel: (91) 11 4176 1620; Fax: (91) 11 4176 1630; www.hayhouse.co.in

Text © Sandy Yawn, 2023

Project editor: Melody Guy • *Indexer:* Joan Shapiro
Cover design: Jeff Miller/Faceout Studio • *Interior design:* Nick C. Welch

The moral rights of the author have been asserted.

A catalogue record for this book is available from the British Library.

Tradepaper ISBN: 978-1-83782-015-3
Hardback ISBN: 978-1-4019-6768-0
E-book ISBN: 978-1-4019-6769-7
Audiobook ISBN: 978-1-4019-6770-3

This product uses papers sourced from responsibly managed forests. For more information, see www.hayhouse.co.uk.

MIX
Paper | Supporting
responsible forestry
FSC® C171272

Printed and bound by CPI Group (UK) Ltd, Croydon CR0 4YY

For Leah Rae, who taught me Grace.

CONTENTS

INTRODUCTION

The winds were starting to gust as we pulled in to Peter Island. This British Virgin Islands port is especially tricky, because it's a narrow passageway, and you must take a sharp left as soon as you're inside the harbor, then pull up to the dock starboard side. There's zero room for error. The marina couldn't fit a vessel any bigger than the one I was captaining. The wind started howling against the hull to the point where it felt as though we could be blown right onto the dock. Yet I had to get this superyacht safely docked with a full load of guests on board. They had lunch plans onshore, after all!

We were surrounded by other boats. Scot Fraser, my first mate on the stern, was making sure the fenders were in place and anxiously communicating over the VHF radio the distances I had to maneuver from bow to stern.

"Okay, Captain, it's two feet to the dock, one and a half feet, now you've got a half foot back here . . . "

Feet shrank to inches until we were finally in place and the spring lines were secured. Amazed, Scot ran up to me.

"Wow, Captain, I've never seen anyone walk the boat like that before. That was awesome!"

"I was hoping that your distances were spot on, and they were," I replied. "Excellent job!"

Walking the boat is the term we use for slowly and carefully moving a vessel from side to side toward its berth. If you need to move three feet to the right, for example, you turn the rudder to the right, then you put the starboard right throttle forward and the port left throttle astern back, then thrust your bow to the right as if to pivot to the left, opposing the engines, turning and throttling as you slide your way in. Except that's not exactly what I was doing.

"You know, Scot, I was actually walking it *away* from the dock," I told him.

The wind was pushing so hard that I needed to slow the momentum. I had to use the conditions I was given and work with them, pushing against the power of the wind to get to where I wanted to go. Scot, who later went on to get his own superyacht captain qualifications, took away from this experience that you must work with whatever momentum you have, turning and pivoting even to the point where you're going in the opposite direction of your desired destination. Or, as Scot shared with me years later:

"Even though you know where you're going, you need to go the other way to get there at the right time."

That is just one of the many lessons I've learned from the stormy seas of my unconventional life and career. As the most seasoned captains—and leaders—know, anything is navigable with the right approach. No storm is too strong, and no wave is too high. When you have the humility to accept the conditions you've been dealt and develop the skill set to work with them, you'll be empowered to chart your own course and get there, even if you are forced to face a few detours.

It sure wasn't a straight line to my position at the helm today. On paper, no one would believe this high school dropout and addict from Florida's backwoods, who cycled in and out of jail and rehab, could ever become captain of some of the world's most exclusive and expensive superyachts, cruising through stunning destinations in the Mediterranean, the Caribbean, and the Middle East with billionaires, CEOs, and celebrities. Yet here I am.

Countless times I have found myself in the middle of the Mediterranean at the end of a grueling day taking care of charter guests, sitting on the bridge, and looking up at the stars during a midnight watch. The only sources of light are the constellations, the moon, the occasional falling star, and the glow from my radar. The rest is inky blackness. It's in those moments I need to pinch myself. It's surreal! I am so filled with gratitude that I get to be there in that moment, alone at the helm of my vessel, captain of my own small, stunning universe.

It's been an epic journey to get to my position. All that I had gone through professionally and personally has equipped me with the necessary calm, confidence, alertness, quick action, and élan to guide my vessel through the most violent storms. More often than not, I've been blessed with the aid of great teams—men and women of character who invested in their training and were prepared to jump in and do whatever was necessary to ensure the safety of our ship and crew. I've also benefitted from the accumulation of experiences that gave me the clarity and resolve to lead through the uncertainty and fear, beginning with my personal story, the dysfunction and abuse of my childhood, the incarcerations and challenges of drug and alcohol addiction, and what led me to decide to build a career at sea in the first place.

I spent my teen and young adult years scrubbing decks on yachts and cleaning the bottoms of boats at a shipyard in Bradenton, Florida. At 25, after getting sober, I landed my first job as member on a boat crew in Fort Lauderdale, which led me to attend Sea School, studying hard to attain all certifications necessary to become a captain. I earned every single one of those stripes on my epaulettes. When you are scraping barnacles off a boat's backside, you are literally working your way from the bottom up. But I found joy in the daily grunt work because I knew that I was taking the necessary steps toward achieving my goal. The point is that anyone can accomplish their heart's desire when they make up their minds, put in the work, remaining teachable, and are never afraid to ask for the help that's always available to them when they look for it.

It is my hope that this book will inspire readers to equip themselves with the qualities of self-leadership that will give them the confidence to answer the call to adventure, whether on sea or on land. It takes a certain kind of person to be okay with sailing away from everyone and everything in their lives for months at a time. It takes a level of courage to be willing to step away from the familiar. The yachties I've had the privilege to lead as captain are often young, or maybe they are just young at heart and hungry for adventure, but they are undeniably a unique breed. I am especially inspired by the famous advertisement that the great explorer Sir Ernest Shackleton is said to have put out in search of the right people for his famous Antarctic expedition:

"Men wanted for hazardous journey.

Low wages, bitter cold, long hours of complete darkness.

Safe return doubtful. Honor and recognition in
event of success."

Yet people answered the ad! Because there will always be this hunger for adventure, to do something that falls outside the bounds of the beaten path that we are all expected to follow. There will always be people excited by the possibilities, who heed that call of the unknown, or discovery. No matter what career path you choose, do it in this spirit of adventure! But first, invest in yourself. Put in the time to build yourself up into the confident leader you are destined to become.

This book will show you how to do that, beginning with the foundational steps necessary for realizing a level of self-leadership that can help you chart your own course toward greatness. Captaining a yacht is a job like no other. It requires a deep grounding and self-actualization, that willingness to work on yourself to the point where you have true confidence. With this self-knowledge in the captain's back pocket, there is no need to rely on classical hierarchy or pull rank. The sense of command is inherent. They radiate authority when they live and breathe the principles of self-leadership. I don't need to reassert my position with every interaction. I get better results when I treat members of my crew as teammates, not peons. They already know I am their captain. But I must earn their respect as a person. At the same time, there must always be respect for the position.

It starts with accountability, a principle that I must live by as captain of a luxury yacht. Legally, ethically, and financially, as captain

I am personally responsible for everything that happens, whether it's physical damage to the vessel or the safety of my passengers and crew. Even if the engine's on fire or a storm is heading our way, I am also responsible for showing the guests a good time.

I deal with a unique mixture of high and low, combining the skills and responsibilities of a military officer handling life and death situations, while also making sure that the sheets are turned down. No task is too menial as I stoop to conquer. Meanwhile, it's incumbent upon me to remain cool under pressure and be present for our high-net-worth passengers, graciously handling complaints if their steak is overcooked or the Jet Ski won't start. If a passenger tells me there weren't enough shrimp in her shrimp cocktail, I can't say, "Sorry, ma'am, I'm too busy trying to keep us afloat!"

I sit at the helm of an enterprise that includes a five-star restaurant, a luxury floating hotel, and an amusement park full of toys and equipment that can cost six figures or more if they get damaged. The bridge is like the White House's situation room, where it all goes down. It's where I must make critical decisions about where and when to sail because of weather. I manage complex multimillion-dollar budgets, shipyard repairs, and charter broker relationships, with VIP clientele dropping as much as $1 million a week for a charter. I am like the CEO of my own company, except that I don't have a team that handles HR, legal, and finance. I do it all myself, so there's little room for error when it comes to the day-to-day operations of a superyacht. I take the time to invest and support a capable and experienced crew. But if things go wrong, someone must shoulder the responsibility, and that person is me.

The stories I will share are intended to inspire you to step up, both for yourself and those around you. My mission is to instill hope and break down the boundaries that hold people back, whether it be naysayers or negative self-talk, by applying the leadership skills and critical thinking inherent to being a captain to empower anyone to navigate their way to a successful life.

Even though many of the adventures I will be sharing culminate thousands of miles away in a place most of you will never see, in a world most will never experience, they transcend setting. They challenge us to look inward and ponder how we would handle ourselves in such dire circumstances. Because everyone experiences a moment in life when they need to lead. Sometimes it's a team, sometimes it's a company, a classroom, a patient ward, a family, or simply yourself. By relating the leadership skills and critical thinking inherent to being a captain, this book will empower you to navigate your way to a successful and more meaningful life. Nothing tests character quite like being tossed like a cork in the middle of the high seas.

Of course, in this context, "captaining" is only partially about being at the helm of a megayacht and everything to do with your own indomitable spirit and personal modus operandi. As William Ernest Henley states in the poem "Invictus": "I am the master of my fate, I am the captain of my soul." I want you to be unafraid to take responsibility for yourself, taking charge of your journeys and boldly choosing the uncharted paths, wherever they may lead.

On these next pages, you will learn about my most chaotic and character-defining moments to lay out the stakes for putting in the work and earning your own stripes. I describe how I overcame a troubled youth and developed the determination to become the leader I am today. Heck, I was the family black sheep with a string of arrests and an unhealthy fondness for tequila that laid waste the first part of my youth, yet look at me now! If I can rise to the top of my industry, my readers can also excel. From my AA sponsor in the 12-step program that saved my life, to the man who hired me and paid for my navigational training, someone always believed in me, and I now believe in the fans of my reality show *Below Deck Mediterranean* who write to me hundreds of messages weekly on social media.

From these interactions I've learned that, with so much fear and uncertainty that surrounded the COVID-19 pandemic, economic hardship, and social unrest, at the time of writing this people have been feeling adrift. Whether a single mom needing words of encouragement as she struggles to make ends meet, an LGBTQ college graduate wondering if there is a place for him in the more traditional industry he dreams about joining, or a corporate executive concerned about becoming a more effective manager to her team, I take the time to answer everyone. I give them essentially the same advice I share with my crew: that investing in your own personal and professional growth are the crucial first steps toward becoming the kind of leader who can bring out the best in others, whether you are captaining a yacht, managing the unit of a corporation, or simply taking care of your own family.

The overarching message is this: When you learn the art of self-leadership—self-discipline, persistence, humility, willingness to change, gratitude, and faith—you, too, will be able to sail through any challenge. Though you may not realize it now, when you have done that inner work, when you've taken the time to learn, improve, and grow, you will be able to reach deep inside yourself and find all the strength, compassion, and tenacity you need.

It will take self-awareness, a willingness to recognize your strengths and weaknesses, and the humility to become teachable. It is never easy to break old habits, avoid past triggers, or throw away a mindset that no longer serves you. But reaching that level of self-mastery is so worth it! You will become the captain of your soul, and that resolve and confidence will naturally radiate outward to the people around you, giving you the foundation to become a great and inspiring leader in any industry, setting, or circumstance.

Now I am inviting you on a journey at sea, loosely following the arc of a typical charter. Within that framework, l will outline my principles of accountability, integrity, communication, attention to detail, and mentorship through the unique lens of a life and career aboard luxury superyachts. I want you to view each chapter as a kind of building block, bringing home each lesson organically with engaging, entertaining, and sometimes shocking anecdotes that demonstrate the art of self-mastery within the context of a life and career at sea as well as a few situations onshore. These principles will be distilled in bulleted takeaways for you to digest at the end of each chapter in a section called "Captain Sandy's Log."

The one through line in all the anecdotes I will share with you is my optimism and abiding faith that, given the right tools and opportunities, individuals are capable of so much more than they realize, especially when they can find someone to believe in them, and I vow to be that person for you. But the ultimate promise of these pages is that you can and should look to yourself for affirmation as a leader in business and in life. Being the captain of one's own soul is within anyone's reach.

Chapter 1

TRUE NORTH

Difficulties are just things to overcome, after all.

—ERNEST SHACKLETON

They don't call the entrance to the Red Sea the "Gates of Hell" for nothing.

After a 4:30 a.m. start at Port Said on the northern end of the Suez Canal, where as many as a hundred vessels transit out of the Mediterranean daily, we chugged along at eight knots on what is possibly the most boring stretch of water on the globe. But this was just phase one of our trip. The plan was to deliver my boss's brand new, 157-foot yacht to Dubai south through the Red Sea, past the Gulf of Aden, then up along the coast of Yemen and Oman in the Arabian Sea to the United Arab Emirates—a 20-day journey of 4,997 nautical miles that would get us there before the end of Ramadan. It was November 2004, a year into the U.S. war with Iraq and numerous other skirmishes across Northern Africa and the Middle East. But no matter—one of the world's wealthiest had some celebrating to do, and I did not want to disappoint.

After crossing the Mediterranean from the South of France at top speed, that 120-mile leg through the canal felt achingly slow, with an undercurrent of tension that was not helped by the fact that the Egyptian pilots who controlled these waters regarded a female captain with a degree of suspicion and disdain.

I knew the score. The previous day my crew and I had taken the hour and a half drive from the port to Giza to tour the pyramids.

The day trip came to an abrupt end when my chef, a tough-as-nails South African woman named Deborah, started shouting at a man who was beating his wife next to one of the monuments. It was horrifying and wrong, but in that part of the world men have the law on their side. I had to stop my chef before she created an international incident and got herself badly hurt in the process.

"Get back on your donkey before you get us all arrested!" I ordered.

Like it or not, when you are just passing through a place you must set your feelings aside and adjust to the local conditions. When you are surrounded by the unfamiliar, it's no one else's job to make you feel at home. That's why I took it in stride when one of the Suez pilots kept shaking his head in disbelief that I, a woman, was captain.

"Look, sir," I calmly told him. "It's going to be okay. I know how to drive a boat."

AUTO PILOT

There was no eye contact or chit chat with me as there was with my male crew. I was used to being a rarity in my industry, and confident in my training and skills, I refused to take it personally. The pilot didn't know any different. Instead I focused on the task in front of me, to receive his instructions and get us through, with plenty of cartons of duty-free cigarettes at the ready in order to ease our interactions with local officials whenever necessary, which was most of the time.

I took turns with members of my crew on the bridge in two-hour shifts. Each one carefully followed the instructions of the pilot: "Two degrees to starboard, four degrees to port . . ." The Suez Canal is a long, skinny channel, so the only way to steer through is straight. I don't blame the pilots. They had to justify getting paid. But whenever it was my turn at the helm, I discretely turned on the auto pilot, moving the wheel as I was told to give him a face-saving show.

Eight hours later, with nothing to look at but sand and oilfields, we reached the end of that flat, two- to three-mile-wide line of water. Now I was ready to do some real navigation. As we said good-bye to our last guide at the Suez Port on the southern end of the canal, I was shocked to hear the pilot say, "See, this is why the captain is the captain. She knows how to steer a straight course!"

He had no idea how right he was!

In the following chapters, I'm going to share with you a multitude of business leadership lessons I've drawn from my years at sea. I begin with the story of the Red Sea because so much of what I now understand as a leader played out during that journey. But if you take away one single piece of wisdom from all the storms and swells endured with humility and described on these pages, it's this: *know your true north.*

We keep all kinds of navigational equipment on a ship, but it's the gyrocompass that keeps us going in the right direction, even when we get turned around by the most violent seas. The gyrocompass has scope that enables it to continuously seek the direction of true geographic north. With all the competing electromagnetic forces of these devices we keep on the bridge, we can get thrown off the course we have charted for ourselves. But this expensive and ingenious device functions by seeking an equilibrium direction under the combined effects of gravitational pull and the daily rotation of the Earth.

That's what we need to embed in ourselves as leaders. A gyrocompass. There are near- and long-term goals when you're running a corporation. You hold regular strategy meetings and obsess about P&L statements every quarter. But it's that innate sense of direction toward what's right and true that keeps you on course. The corporate term for this is "purpose." Your ability to attract talent and investment dollars, to engage their workforce and consumers, the state of your long-term health as a business depends on it. Besides, how can you lead others without a sense of direction? If you want others to follow, knowing your true north is a prerequisite.

As I write this, CEOs who haven't yet come up with an overall mission statement are spending millions on consultants as they scramble to develop something overarching that is both authentic and inspiring. And those who have a pamphlet of "company values" gathering dust on a shelf are asking themselves who they are and what they really stand for. They're in the throes of creating a living, breathing document that can rally their people and give them that shared sense of purpose that underpins all they do.

When first I embarked on my Red Sea journey, I thought my purpose was to deliver a superyacht to its owner intact and in time for his Ramadan celebrations. Little did I know how much higher that sense of mission would go. My true north was about to have a major reset.

CHAMPAGNE CORK

The canal opened into the Gulf of Suez, a 200-mile-long rift with the distant red rocks of Mount Sinai piercing the azure blue skies on our port side, and southern Egypt's parched landscape on our starboard side. Within a couple of hours, we started to feel the churn, and by the time we hit the more open waters of the Red Sea we were getting pounded by 8- to 10-foot swells. Our luxury superyacht, *White Star*, one of the largest vessels under my command to date, was getting tossed around like a cork in one of the bottles of the champagne for which it was named.

The yacht's previous owner, entrepreneur and investor John Flynn, was well aware that *White Star* was also the name of the shipping line for the *Titanic*. It was the name he gave to all of his boats. (He loved that champagne best, though he named his wave runners *Moet* & *Chandon*.) My new boss, an Arabian businessman who hired me when we did the boat build, seemed equally indifferent to the implications for his new toy. Maybe that was my first sign that I should not have left the dock. This was a brand-new vessel that had traveled straight out of the New Orleans shipyard by transport ship to the port of Toulon in France, from where I ran it to Antibes. It was completely untested by rough seas, so I worried about whether the engines were mounted securely into the beds of the hull, just as a pilot of a brand-new airplane might fret over the welding on its first flight. *Will the wings stay on?*

It was a tricky call for me as a leader. There are always forces above you, and in the hierarchy of the maritime industry, or any other business, for that matter, certain expectations must be met.

A board member may hang conditions on an investment you don't entirely agree with, for example, while a boat owner wants what he wants when he wants it, regardless of the conditions at sea. It's up to you to make that calculation, choosing between pressure to deliver and that little nagging voice of doubt in the back of your head. You make that call, then you mitigate the risks as best you can.

So we pushed ahead. As the waves continued to slam headlong into us, making the entire vessel shudder on our shakedown cruise, I noticed we were taking on water. This was not normal on a superyacht. Decks have drains that channel the water back over the side, so this should not have been happening. I slowed down the boat and sent Derrick, my first officer, to the bow to check the chain locker— the compartment from which we hoist or drop the anchor and chains.

"Strap yourself in and put on your life jacket, Derrick, I want to see where we are taking on water," I told him.

Keep in mind, the boat was being tossed up and down, hard. I was terrified that Derrick might bump his head as he peered down one of the lockers. Over the radio, I could hear him vomiting. Even the most seasoned yacht crew can suffer seasickness in those conditions, which feel like you are trapped inside an elevator with some angry giant jerking the cable up and down several floors at a time.

"What do you see, Derrick? Where's the water coming from?" I asked him.

He quickly discovered that one of the deck drains hadn't been welded properly. Instead of draining overboard, the water was going into the locker. Somehow, in between heaving his guts out, Derrick was able to stuff a line in the hole to slow the flow of water into the chain locker until we could get to port to make the necessary repairs.

AN INAUSPICIOUS START

Three days prior to arriving in Port Said, while we were still crossing the Mediterranean, I got a call on the ship's satellite phone. It was the parents of one of my crew members—a sweet, 21-year-old kid from New Zealand—calling to let him know that his

19-year-old sister had been killed in a car accident. I will never forget his stricken face, knowing from that moment on, his life would never be the same.

You take care of your people above all else. As a captain, I am responsible for the well-being of my crew beyond their voyage at sea. It's also my job to see them safely home, so it was my priority to get this guy on a plane back to his family as soon as humanly possible. Again, this was Ramadan and much of Egypt had been shut down, so I had to scramble to find a travel agency that was open and could book him reliable transportation to Cairo and onto the first flight available to Auckland.

At this point we were about 20 hours from the nearest port. It must have been the longest 20 hours of my grieving crew member's young life. The water was smooth as glass as we cruised southward. Strangely, a little yellow bird was following us the whole way. Funny how the smallest things can stick in your memory. I'd never seen anything like that so far out at sea. Maybe it was a sign from my deckhand's baby sister. The other signs weren't nearly as auspicious. Death, flooding, and violent sea swells—what the heck was I thinking?

Here I was, a petite, 34-years-young female captain, at the helm of the largest vessel I had ever run. When I first learned about the assignment, I had been excited for the adventure. *This ought to be interesting,* I had thought. My boat had practically doubled in size from a 92-foot Hatteras worth $10 million to 157-foot motor yacht worth $60 million. I went from managing a crew of 4 to 12 overnight.

It wasn't easy to find these individuals. Our chosen route to Dubai was admittedly dangerous, but there really were no safe alternatives from our point of departure. When my newly hired officers, deckhands, and stews found out our destination, two-thirds of them quit.

"This is not what I signed up for," one of them told me as he picked up his duffel bag and walked down the dock.

The core team members, including Brad, my engineer; Derrick, my first officer; and Chef Denise, stayed with me. But I had to scramble to find replacement crew at the last minute and, though most of the last-minute hires were seasoned in life experience, their yachting resumes were not entirely traditional. Our insurance company also required us to hire someone whose expertise could not be further from the world of luxury yachting: an ex-member of British special forces named Sean.

Looking like one of those action-movie heroes with the thousand-yard stare, Sean was to be my security consultant on the trip. He was chosen for his extensive knowledge of the Middle East, his contacts and ability to identify hotspots. He would be monitoring our radio for pirate activity and coaching our team on actions to take to minimize their exposure in the event we were attacked or boarded. If he had any skepticism about my own qualifications for this job, he kept it well hidden. Meanwhile, I quickly came to appreciate his understanding of the region, as well as his bone-dry English wit.

Sean's presence on the ship was reassuring. In fact, everyone on board was clear about what their roles were, and I'd made a point about communicating with everyone clearly and often. As leader, I can never assume that everyone is on the same page, or that crucial information is getting properly disseminated. I make a point of looking everyone in the eye, making sure they acknowledge the message—leaving no room for the possibility that misinformation can break down the cohesiveness of my team. In a short space of time, my crew had attained that necessarily level of clarity and mutual understanding. It added to my confidence in what we were about to undertake, despite the inherent risks.

As leader, I can never assume that everyone is on the same page, or that crucial information is getting properly disseminated. I make a point of looking everyone in the eye, making sure they acknowledge the message—leaving no room for the possibility that misinformation can break down the cohesiveness of my team.

The responsibility for everyone's safety fell to me. And I had accepted this challenge during the region's holiest of holidays. Like those pounding waves, the reality of the risks involved finally hit me on that Red Sea voyage. I had 12 souls on board, minus the deckhand I'd sent home to grieve with his family. If anything were to happen to a member of my team, I'd never forgive myself. By now we had another two weeks in these waters to go, and I was feeling the full weight of my command.

As we continued southward, it wasn't long before those roiling seas led to hydraulics failure and engine trouble. One of the engines was overheating, so we had to shut it down and limp along at five knots. By then we were close to the Gulf of Aden, where the Red Sea narrows between the African country of Eritrea to the west and Yemen to the east. We had to get to calm water so that Brad could work safely on the engines, but where? I'd hired another experienced captain to join me on this trip, someone who'd worked on the Disney Magic cruise ship. Derrick was thrilled to be off the milk run, doing some real navigation in a boat that didn't feel like a floating building block. I asked him for some options.

"Options!" he shouted back at me enthusiastically before turning to scrutinize the radar.

HELL *AND* HIGH WATER

It's not like any of the alternatives were good. We could either make our way to the coast of Eritrea on the west or Yemen to the east. Both places were known to be rife with human rights abuses and political volatility that made them potentially dangerous for outsiders. In fact, the whole region was a tinderbox, with cells of al-Qaeda and its allied extremists located in almost every country whose waters we were passing through. But Yemen would be less of a detour. Peering at the radar, my "first officer" spotted a small island of that country's southern coast that would have to do.

This was just two days after George W. Bush had been re-elected. When there is a president-elect making world news headlines—an individual who brought war to parts of the region during his first term—people don't discriminate, no matter which way you voted.

There were also rumors that Yasser Arafat, then chairman of the Palestine Liberation Organization, had died, making the region even more of a tinderbox. Adding to our perils was the fact that pirates were a constant threat.

You may remember a wave of news stories years back in which piracy was an especially big concern in parts of the world such as the Red Sea, the Horn of Africa, and the Indian Ocean. That year there were 329 pirate attacks reported around the world, and they were starting to spike in those waters. Pirates don't go after someone because they're American or because of nationality. They aren't interested your country; they just want your money. They are thieves at sea, with little to no allegiance to ideologies or territories. So, whether you have an American flag flying from out on your yacht or not, they're still going to look at your vessel and size you up for an attack.

That's why it was imperative that we get this luxury yacht off the high seas, where it was a slow-moving target. We chugged along the next 80 miles, finally setting our anchor at 3 a.m. Around 6 a.m. we woke to the sound of boats surrounding us. We had dropped our hook at a Yemen military camp, anchoring in an unauthorized military zone. It wasn't marked on the chart, but I wasn't going to argue that fact.

Our intention was to do nothing but leave as soon as our repairs were completed. Now I'm a pretty seasoned traveler. Again, I operate under the idea that it is not the job of a foreign country to make you feel comfortable, it's to make its own people feel comfortable. But this was way past uncomfortable. Before we were boarded, I had my first disagreement with Sean.

"Sandy, you and the other women need to hide yourselves, now. I'll pretend to be the captain."

"No way!" I told him. "This is part of my job!"

"It's not part of your job to get yourself beaten, raped, or killed!"

He had a point. I didn't like it one bit, but humbling myself and taking direction from a security expert who knew the risks and how we could protect ourselves was the best decision I could have made as leader in that moment. Making myself a target would have endangered everyone, putting the boat and crew in even greater peril. Good leadership is also about knowing your limitations. Even when you are in charge you must be willing to listen, take direction, and partner with someone with different skill sets and experience from your own.

By now I was beginning to realize that my real purpose on this journey, my true north, wasn't getting to our destination so much as it was protecting the lives and well-being of all souls on board. Getting there required me to think about the team around me, acknowledging that I didn't have all the answers and being okay with asking for or receiving help.

I made sure that all the women, all five of us, were hidden deep below deck, locked inside a compartment with a door disguised by wood paneling, while these guys with machine guns walked the boat to inspect it.

At this point one crew member, who was American, wanted to claim that he was Canadian. *Are you kidding me?*

"Man up!" I told him.

"But Captain, they hate Americans here!"

"For God's sake, you are from Los Angeles and you sound like a surfer dude. Who do you think you are fooling? Trust me, they don't care where you are from. If they want to highjack the vessel and take us hostage, they are not going to leave the Canadian!"

THIS IS NOT A DRILL

I was pretty sure it was just the shiny new boat and all its equipment they'd be interested in and not our nationalities, the day's geopolitics aside. We just needed to fix the boat and fast. Naturally the men on the gunboats were suspicious of this opulent ship that had suddenly appeared in their midst. One of my senior male crew managed to find someone who spoke enough English to help him explain the situation to the Yemeni officers and, thankfully, they left us to it. Five days later, we finished the repairs and hauled anchor. As we rounded the island, we high-fived each other in celebration of not getting detained as hostages or worse.

Our elation didn't last long. About 15 minutes into our journey, the bridge phone rang. It was Brad, the chief engineer.

"Fire!" he yelled. "The whole engine room is in flames!"

Right after Brad spoke these words, the entire vessel lost power. Flames were coming out of the exhaust when a giant fireball suddenly ripped through the engine room.

Derrick asked me if he should pull the C02 fire extinguisher.

"Nooooooo!" I screamed. "Absolutely not!"

Brad was in the engine room. The C02 extinguisher, which works by displacing the oxygen that is feeding a fire, could have killed him in such a confined space.

"As my first officer it's your job to be my eyes and ears," I reminded Derrick. "You go to the scene of the fire, then report back to me just like you were trained to, and do nothing until I give the order."

I could not have been more emphatic. Coincidentally, the day before we had a fire drill for all crew. Drills are a regular occurrence on the boats I captain. As leader, it's my job to prepare everyone for what may or may not come to pass. You can never train enough. We owe it to ourselves and the people under us to continually refresh and upgrade our knowledge and abilities on the job. I rally the crew, encouraging them and giving them all the tools they need to handle any situation. I remain calm and reassure them that we are going to be okay, although I do level with them so that they can join me on the journey with their eyes wide open. To some extent that training helped. Repeat the drill often enough and it stays in your mental muscle memory, allowing you to go on autopilot, focusing on what you need to do. But so many other things can happen in a crisis situation that you could never prepare for.

PIRATE BAIT

We were now completely adrift, carrying millions of dollars' worth of equipment. If we still had any hope of making it to Dubai as originally planned, they fizzled in that moment. Our engines were completely destroyed. After learning about the fire, a stew from the Philippines panicked and tried to jump overboard. I grabbed her, pulled her inside, and sat her down, reassuring her that we would get the fire under control, which we did. But now what? The Red Sea was still pounding as we drifted toward the Yemen coast.

How many times have you felt as if your business was being attacked by pirates, maybe in the form of competition, or a negative review gone viral over social media? And how many times has going into panic mode helped you to manage these threats? If anything, it's led to decisions that have made things worse. Fear is a reaction. Courage is a decision. Again, in the middle of that Red Sea chaos I made the conscious choice to put on a calm demeanor. The one thing you don't do as a leader is show you're scared. You need to instill confidence in order to get others to follow. When asked what makes a great leader, the late General Colin Powell shared something his sergeant back in infantry in Fort Benning told him:

"One day, lieutenant, you'll know you're a good leader when people follow you, if only out of curiosity."

Your people have to trust you, but you have to build up that trust through self-possession and self-leadership, and many other things, such as serving selflessly, sharing the risks and the load, and providing them the training and the resources to get the job done. And, above all, never let them see you look cold, or tired, or hungry, or terrified. Only then, when your own conduct has earned their trust, will they "follow you into the darkest night, the largest waves and the narrowest channels."

With no engine power and dangers coming at us from all sides, you bet I was terrified. But my crew couldn't see it on my face or hear it in my voice, and that calm telegraphed to them that the situation was somehow manageable. If we took certain steps and maintained focus, we would be all right.

Back on the bridge, the first officer, engineer, and I met to discuss what had just happened and what to do next. Derrick put his hand on Brad's shoulder and said, "This guy saved the ship," before boasting about how he'd pulled the C02.

Derrick must have panicked after I'd expressly told him not to, but Brad was enraged.

"You mean all that smoke billowing through the control room was C02?!" Brad asked him. "You could have killed me!"

Then Brad lunged for Derrick. I had to jump in between the two men to stop them from coming to blows while the boat was tossing back and forth.

As all this was happening, my head of security, Sean, kindly informed me that there were pirates in the vicinity. Well of course there were! Yachts are especially vulnerable to theft in certain seas. We tow expensive boats about 100 feet behind us, so all a thief needs to do is get in at the right time with a pair of bolt cutters. Yachts going through dicey waters have been known to wrap themselves in razor wire.

Owners have also hired private security with machine guns, though insurers don't like the practice because the last thing you want to get into is a firefight at sea. Beyond that, each country has its own rules about carrying weapons, which you must declare upon entering their waters. Some countries can confiscate your whole yacht if they find weapons. Others may have you surrender them while you are voyaging through their waters, which defeats the purpose. Some captains and owners get around this by hiding their weapons inside secret storage spaces, but it's not worth the risk.

I've never allowed guns on board and never will. Being overly aggressive or reactive is rarely a good strategy. The best way to handle risk or threats is by strictly following the maritime safety protocols and using my wits. When there is the threat of pirates, you first call the Coast Guard. Then you zigzag your course (the one time it actually is okay to veer from true north), lighting up your boat and showing presence on deck with as many bodies as possible, bringing out the fire hoses and charging the pirates with sea water if they are in range. It's a way of letting them know you are well aware of their presence to hopefully deter them from approaching your vessel. By then they most likely realize that you have contacted the Coast Guard, the Navy, and any other ships in the area to alert them that you are under attack. Today, there are also long-range acoustic devices that will blow out the eardrums of any pirate who gets close enough. But that day on the Red Sea, I had none of the above.

I did have our secret weapon, Sean, who was a true badass. He had trained us well. I knew he would be on the case, allowing me to focus on what was right in front of me, which was a lot. That was the kind of moment when it became so apparent why I hire for character and not skills or work history. Because there is really no way to prepare for how you will react at that moment until it arrives.

A VOICE IN THE DARK

Moments before Sean's warning, I had radioed a nearby warship, and it appeared some enterprising pirates had heard my distress signal.

After the attacks of September 11, 2001, NATO formed a coalition of warships to monitor the Red Sea and other parts of the world. As we were making our way through the Gulf of Suez, during my night watch on the bridge, I remembered hearing an American woman's voice on the radio of one of these ships, breaking through the silence. She was asking boats to radio in with their names, coordinates, and destination as part of the security monitoring process, and I'd noticed that none of the captains were responding back to her. Yet when one of her male officers radioed the same question, they were answered immediately. It annoyed me.

I remember thinking to myself, *One day this will change if more women join the maritime industry.*

That dispatcher's voice stuck in my mind, so that was the warship I decided to call when it was clear we were in serious trouble:

"Warship 68, I'm an American citizen, I have sustained a catastrophic fire. I have 12 souls on board, and we are drifting inside northern Yemen territory."

The warship replied with the due diligence of questions, and I answered all of them between containing one crew member from jumping overboard and stopping two crew members from killing each other. So much was happening in the space of a few minutes that many details are a blur. But what has stayed with me all these years later was the words from that warship's captain.

"You are our priority, and you will remain our priority until you are in a safe port," he told me.

The lesson here is that you are never entirely out of options. There is always hope. As you look around, you may not immediately see the solution in the inky, heaving waters of the crisis you are trying to manage or lead your way out of. Yet there are always resources you can pull or calls you can make to solve a problem. When you've paid attention, that past conversation, piece of data, or name will bubble up from the recesses of your memory and reveal itself right in your moment of greatest need. Have faith!

Of course, we weren't there yet. The warship was still some distance away, and by then it was clear our situation was extremely perilous. Floating off the coast of Yemen, we were more than a little conspicuous in our gleaming white, multimillion-dollar luxury motor yacht. Our trip across the Mediterranean and through the Suez Canal up to this point had not exactly been smooth sailing, but at least we had a functioning engine. Now, after a fireball blew through the exhaust on the portside of the vessel, leaving a big, charred hole on the main deck, we had no power, making us sitting ducks for any enterprising pirates who happened to hear my distress call on the radio. And they did.

When you lose power, you should still have enough stored in the satellite phone battery for 24 hours of communication.

"Grab a pen and paper!" I told my sister Michelle, blurting out my coordinates.

"What are you talking about?" she asked.

"It's our last known position, in case they need to find our bodies," I explained. "We sustained a fire and we're okay, but we're still in danger. There are 13 of us floating in Yemen territory and a warship is on its way. If you don't hear back from me in half an hour, call the U.S. Embassy, it means we've been taken hostage."

"Sis, get your ass home now!" Michelle wailed. "I'm tired of having to worry about you!"

"I'm trying, believe me!" I said.

I knew that we had done all we could to secure ourselves and our vessel. Now we just had to sit tight and wait. It felt like forever.

"Now let's see who gets here first—the pirates or the warship?" Sean wisecracked.

It was the one time I did not appreciate his wry sense of humor. After four tense hours, a U.S. Navy warship finally appeared over the horizon, flying the American flag. It did not occur to me until later that this destroyer had nearly been the object of an attack by al-Qaeda suicide bombers in these very waters. The attack failed because the bomb that was strapped onto the boat was so heavy that it sank before it could leave the port. But a year later, in 2000, the same group succeeded on a sister ship, killing 17 U.S. Navy personnel and injuring 39 while the vessel was being refueled in Yemen's Aden harbor. It was the USS *Cole*.

The sacrifices of our U.S. Armed Forces in the region were only just beginning. I felt a surge of gratitude for these men and women in uniform. There had been some grumbling among the crew members about America, especially from the wannabe Canadian. But that cynicism stopped as soon as the Navy came to the rescue. I had never felt so proud to be an American in my life when that gorgeous destroyer rolled up and told us, "You are under our protection now!"

The Navy captain's next words were:

"That's some exit wound you've got there," referring to the gaping black hole left in our portside hull by the firebomb that ripped through our exhaust port.

One of the officers asked me where I wanted to be towed to.

"Florida!" I joked.

OBJECTS OF SUSPICION

Everyone laughed. But our sense of relief didn't last. The next best thing the warship could do was take us to Hodeida, which is the main port in Yemen, where we would spend the next 13 days waiting for a tow back to the safety of the Mediterranean. This did not necessarily mean we had found safe harbor. That year, Yemen was in the first throes of a years-long, bloody civil war. It began with the Houthis in northern Yemen against the Yemeni military before escalating into a full-scale civil war. Like many of these conflicts, there was an ideological aspect to the conflict. The Houthis followed a strict version of Islam. God knows what might have happened to us had we washed up on Yemen's northwestern shores, which was a real possibility. But even in Yemen's more southern port city we were objects of suspicion and hostility.

My next satellite phone call was to my Middle Eastern boss. Because the *White Star* and all its equipment still had the better part of a year under warranty, he arranged for a small army of private security to protect his investment. The shipyard owner we were dealing with was also well-connected, with military contracts all over the region, so we found ourselves surrounded by men with rocket launchers. Not that this gave me total peace of mind. All but one of us was Western, so we stuck out in that dusty provincial outpost, and not in a good way. Our luxury megayacht didn't exactly blend in with our surroundings either.

After we docked, none of us dared leave the protection of those heavily armed guards. But within a few hours we had no choice. Some Yemeni "officials" came by and ordered us to pile into the back of their beat-up Toyota pickup truck, with two AK-47-armed soldiers standing on its tailgate. It wasn't clear if they were there for our protection or to stop us from escaping. And we couldn't be certain if any of the Yemeni officials with whom we were dealing were loyal to the government or the Houthi insurgents.

As we drove through town, we became increasingly convinced that we were about to be taken hostage. Their equivalent of Main Street was a dirt road with no traffic lights or rules, where goats and other livestock were causing traffic jams and donkeys were the main means of transportation. The sight of wild-eyed child and teenage soldiers carrying machine guns gave us chills. This is what happens in a country where people don't have hope. Each one of us was praying. Fortunately, we were merely being taken to the local immigration building for processing.

Later that day, when we were all safely back on board, Sean made some calls. His friend who worked security at the British Embassy in Yemen passed along some chatter he'd heard, which Sean then confirmed from his other intelligence sources. A group of insurgents was heading toward the port town from the north. He had an extraordinary ability to gather and process the facts, then deliver the information in a way that was as calm as it was unambiguous. I've taken a similar approach: I need the full picture before making a judgment or taking an action. And now it was clear we needed to make a move.

"Captain, we need to get you and your crew out of here. This many Westerners in one place puts us on their radar, and the longer we stay together the greater the chance there will be a hostage incident."

As a leader I've taken a similar approach:
I need the full picture before making
a judgment or taking an action.

"What about the boat?" I asked him.

"I'll stay here and see it through," he said.

I called my boss and told him what was up.

"We'll fly everyone out and get them home safe," he told me. "But you're the captain and you must stay with the ship."

Damn! I thought, *Doesn't he realize it's the chef who goes down with the ship?* Although of course I knew he was right.

So Sean and I stayed with the boat, sleeping in shifts: me during the night and Sean during the day. It would take another 13 days for the insurance company to arrange a tow out of there. Meanwhile, I was so sick and weak from malaria that Sean had to carry me to the car that would take us to the airport. As soon as we landed in Dubai, I was greeted by someone from the management company who took one look at me and said, "Captain, you need to see a doctor."

I was rushed to a pediatrician, the only doctor's office in the vicinity that was open during Ramadan. I was told that there were 500 strands of malaria in Yemen, but that it was a good guess I had one of about 100 strands. He then dosed me up with a pharmacy's worth of pills and sent me back to my hotel, where I slept for two days. On my last day in Dubai I went to have tea with the boat's owner, to debrief him on the whole catastrophe.

TEAM EXCELLENCE

A year later, during the Miami International Boat Show, I was awarded the International Superyacht Society's Distinguished Crew Award. Gary Groenewold, who at the time was vice president of Westrec Marina's Southern Region and sponsor of the award, told the audience, "The leadership exuded by the captain reverberated through the crew and provided quiet confidence in them as a team and courage under fire during their hellacious series of events. The captain and crew put their knowledge and skills to work in a situation that could have had a very different ending."

It was one of the proudest moments of my career. But I knew the only reason we'd made it through was because of the cumulative experience and excellence of the team that was with me. I could not have chosen a better group of individuals to get us through that harrowing experience. They didn't all have the classic resumes, but they had the backbone. Everyone understood that we didn't have time to debate whether something was in their job description; it simply had to get done. Crew members of all ranks and roles were fighting flames and preventing injuries. Sure, a few of them had their moments. It was an incredibly tense situation and we're all human. But I'll never forget how they all came together when it counted.

So much of that story's outcome was based on intensive training and experience. Like my crew members, I was able to display calm in the middle of the storm because of all the living and learning I had done up until that moment. It made me the leader I needed to be to ensure that a disaster did not become a tragedy.

A Successful Failure

Sir Ernest Shackleton, the legendary leader of an Antarctic expedition at the beginning of the last century, didn't receive all of his honors and accolades for a successful mission. In fact, the mission to the South Pole was a spectacular failure. The explorer and his crew never managed to carry out their stated goal of traversing the frozen continent from coast to coast on foot, stopping at the South Pole along the way—a distance of around 2,000 miles—because they never even made it to shore. Their ship, Endurance, got trapped and eventually crushed between ice floes 10 feet thick. Overall, the crew had to survive 21 months in the cold before being rescued, enduring whipping polar winds and near starvation. Sir Ernest had to find a way to keep up morale as they set up camp on the ice flow with five small tents, three lifeboats, and 70 sled dogs, most of which they had to kill as they ran out of food for them.

When the ice melted, they moved into lifeboats and sailed to Elephant Island, where they survived by hunting penguins and seals. Then Shackleton and five others set sail for South Georgia Island, surviving 16 days being tossed around on icy waters on an open boat. Conditions there weren't much better in that remote cove where they landed, but Sir Ernest and two other men trekked across mountains, glaciers, and crevasses to the other side, where there was a whaling station. It would take several tries and about three more months under daunting conditions, but Sir Ernest eventually managed to rescue all 28 of the stranded souls and get them back home from Britain. Even the Endurance was found in 2022, 107 years after it sank to the bottom of the Weddell Sea, in amazing condition. What a story of perseverance, faith, and leadership!

My own Red Sea adventure pales by comparison. But my pivot to a mission of survival helped us make it through the ordeal with humor and optimism. I'm proud to say that not once did we give in to despair.

BEYOND BOOK SMART

Of course, this story was about much more than professional training. Leading your team when all around you is uncertainty and chaos also requires life skills and wisdom that are not necessarily covered in a certification course or textbook. One example is communication. Leaders often keep it to themselves. They either forget to share, or they choose to withhold under the misguided intention of protecting the people under them.

Again, whenever I get information, I tell my crew. I never want to hear they weren't informed. And I never want to find out later that an obstacle could have been avoided if they'd kept me in the loop. I'll share more about the importance of this two-way transparency in the coming chapters. So many of the largest problems I've encountered in my world, and I'll wager many of yours, begin with communication. It's absurd to me that we live in a time when we have so much incredible technology at our fingertips, yet our communication skills are so lacking. We spend so much time talking to each other through screens that we can lose our ability to just look another person in the eye and clearly communicate as a human being.

Another tool, something that you acquire through personal growth, is the ability to tune out the noise and find a place of clarity and calm. Through the years, I've done a lot of work on myself, cultivating the ability to not react. In the moment I have learned to pause and ask myself: *Is this coming from emotion, or is this coming from fact?* Then I check in with myself and take that breath.

CHECK YOUR FEET

A friend once told me that, in times of great stress, you should "look at where your feet are." If you take that minute and look at where your feet are and take that breath and you look up at a person, it can change everything. Checking my feet is a centering tool that I often use on land and sea. You cannot let your head take you out. If you do, the stories will grow and grow in your head, and you end up far away from the present moment. When you take a minute to breathe in and look down at your feet, you go, *No, I'm standing here on a boat dealing with this one situation. Focus on what's relevant.* Then I lift my head back up, able to say to the person standing before me, "Give me the facts." Then I base my decision off the data, not the feelings or the fears.

This approach played out when I was rudderless in the sloppy seas, pirates lurking in the distance. It was like watching the scenes of a horror movie slowly unfold. I had to reach deep within my soul to take control of the situation, assess my next moves, and lead my crew. They were petrified and looked to me as the captain of their vessel. I called each one to the bridge by name. As we stood there, I made them look me in the eye and take two deep inhales and exhales of the breath. I reminded each of them of their specific job and what tasks would take priority. Even as the fear was knocking me in the gut, I knew innately I had to be the calm in the middle of that storm.

"We got this," I told them.

There were times on deck and on the bridge in the Red Sea when things went perfectly still and quiet, despite the crashing waves and bombardment of bad news that was coming at me from all sides. That's when the chatter in my brain disappeared. I call it "zero focus" when the only thing in my awareness is the task that must be performed in that exact moment. I call it zero focus and not laser focus because I am so centered, it's as if I've reached some sort of mental ground zero. It's a level of concentration that we can all tap into, enabling us to perform at levels of excellence we never knew possible.

Not that I brought all the above-mentioned wisdom to bear during that harrowing series of incidents on the Red Sea. I have since had more than 20 years of seasoning as a leader, learning through experience and continuous training. I am the eternal student who knows that my advancement in life comes from remaining humble and teachable, acknowledging when I am wrong and how I can do better next time. While I am proud of how I led my crew through crisis after crisis, I did make a couple of mistakes. If I had to endure that situation all over again I would not, for example, have deferred to someone else's opinion while ignoring my own best instincts. When I asked one of my officers where to drop anchor, I had my doubts about the location but leaned on his experience. Then we were boarded. That was on me. As much as I respected my crew, I needed to take more ownership of my decisions as captain.

Later, during the fire, I took the same officer's advice *not* to drop anchor.

"Sandy, we'll never get it back up," he warned me.

Had I trusted my own judgment and dropped the anchor, I'd have slowed the drift, minimizing any further damage caused by the slamming of waves into our vessel. Instead, we were left to lurch back and forth on the violent swell for hours. Again, that was on me as the leader. It was a tough, split-second decision, but it is in those moments that you need to be able to access the self-confidence to move forward with what your gut is telling you. Gather as much information as you can, of course, but trust yourself and be decisive. Never again would I set aside my own best instincts, especially when it concerns the safety of all the souls on board.

One of my biggest regrets was not following up with my crew once we were all out of danger. We were all strangers to each other when I first hired them through a crew agency. But over that two-week period, sharing a lifetime's worth of experiences, we'd gotten to know each other extremely well. And then we all dispersed to our own corners of the world like it never happened.

That's the thing about trauma. At the time you just want to move past it without looking back. You're just thinking about surviving and getting home to your friends and family. I was recently asked if I remained close to Sean, my rock who got me out of Yemen alive. After all, one would think those shared experiences would lead to quite a bond. But I haven't spoken with him since. There was no follow-up after that incident, not even from the management company. For years, it was as if I'd locked my emotions about what had happened inside a safe that I couldn't access. Then, in 2013, I found myself in a movie theater watching *Captain Phillips* with Tom Hanks, about the cargo ship captain whose quick thinking and courage helped him save his crew from Somalian pirates. My reaction was visceral. Suddenly, I was back on that boat and started having a panic attack. Those long-buried emotions were out of the box!

The intense experience on the Red Sea in 2004, at a time when the region was a geopolitical tinderbox, was a career-defining, life-changing moment for me, and a prime example of what happens when leadership is tested by crisis. Again, professional experience had trained me well for that moment, but it was life experience that helped me to respond with the calm and clarity necessary to lead my crew through the some of the scarier moments. I was no stranger to overcoming adversity, having persevered through a tough youth and overwhelming personal loss, each new challenge only building my resilience and strengthening my resolve.

As I write this, we are all experiencing some rough seas. You may well be having your own moments of uncertainty and panic. Maybe you're running a business that has had major disruption from pandemic restrictions, inflation, and supply-chain problems. You've lost a source of income or, far worse, a loved one. You've passed through our own version of Hell's Gate and, as you're being tossed around a figurative Red Sea, have yourself looking for guidance from our politicians and members of the media, only to receive conflicting information from individuals with their own agendas. We are living in an era of unprecedented turmoil, and it often seems like there is no one at the helm with the judgment, credentials, or compassion to give us the right direction. That's why we must learn to navigate this world for ourselves. Again, we must learn to rely on our own inner compass—our true north—for guidance.

Whether on dry land or at sea, you may be wondering how you can become the captain of your own situation, charting the course that's best for you in the middle of all the noise. If you are, keep reading. While I don't claim to have all the answers, there is plenty I can share from my own experiences, as well as the teachings of other leaders I've been blessed to come across on my extensive travels. I'd be honored if you'll allow me to be your captain over these next pages. The fact that you are seeking out tools for self-leadership tells me you are already on your way, and I'd hire you to crew for me any day!

- **Adapt to your local conditions.** Whether you find yourself in a strange land, or are interacting with a different corporate culture, try hard to see things from their point of view. When you are surrounded by the unfamiliar, it's no one else's job to make you feel at home. You'll make more progress when you listen, learn, and make every effort to adjust.

- **Communicate well, and often.** Don't assume that everyone's on the same page, or that crucial information is getting properly disseminated. Look everyone in the eye and make sure they acknowledge the message, leaving no room for the possibility that misinformation can break down the cohesiveness of your team.

- **Drill it in.** You can never train enough. Practice, practice, practice just like you would in any sport. We owe it to ourselves and the people under us to continually refresh and upgrade our knowledge and abilities on the job.

- **Get the facts.** Don't react to an impression. Remember restraint of pen and tongue. A sliver of information is not enough. Gather all the information you can before making a judgment or taking an action.

- **It's all in your approach.** Handle a problem or crisis based on full information while maintaining situational awareness. Defuse any problem you see, then infuse it with a facts-based solution.

- **Humble yourself to learn.** The greatest leaders are always teachable. Seeking information and acknowledging that you don't know everything is not a sign of weakness, it's a superpower. There is no such thing as a dumb question.

- **Look at your feet.** The human mind is full of chatter. We are constantly telling ourselves stories, to the point where the narrative takes over and we lose sight of the simple facts on the ground. That's when panic and overwhelm set in. But small actions can help you press the reset button. Like staring at your shoes for 30 seconds. Or taking a deep breath and counting to 10. Or playing a song that instantly lifts your mood. Experiment to find out what works for you. Empower yourself to snap out of it.

- **Model the professionalism you want to see in others.** If you want to build a culture of respect, you must demonstrate what that looks like in your own behavior. Be it so they can see it.

Chapter 2

ON THE SEA FLOOR

There is no joy like the joy of those who have hit bottom and survived.

—JOAN LARKIN

As we sat together at the front of the school bus, the redhead girl from next door slipped me a little white pill.

"What's this, Heather?" I asked her.

"It's a quaalude, silly," she told me. "Try it. It'll make you feel sooo good!"

It's not that I felt *bad*, necessarily. For the most part I was a happy-go-lucky kid. But even though I was a rules follower who tried my best in school, classes could be boring to the point of torture. My ADHD brain was wired in a way that made it next to impossible to focus within that setting. Michelle's nickname for me was "Squirrel" because I was always chasing after that next delicious nut.

Who knows? I thought to myself as I popped the barbiturate into my mouth. *Maybe this will make the day go by a little faster.*

It didn't. The euphoria they talked about never happened for me. In fact, as we pulled up to the school parking lot, I started to panic.

"Just go with it, Sandy," Heather assured me. "Once it kicks in you will feel so calm."

Homeroom, math, and English passed me by in a blur. The warm, melty feeling Heather promised me never came. Instead it felt weird and out of body, though not in a good way. But I was okay with it, because taking that trip gave me the acceptance of the cool kids I craved. Suddenly, I was one of them. I'd always wanted to fit in, and I didn't have anyone to look up to or guide me. My mom was in the throes of her alcoholism, and my older sisters (Sabrina and Kim) were just as lost as they tried to find their own place in life. Succumbing to peer pressure and popping that pill represented my newfound freedom, or so I thought. I was 13 years old.

FROM THE FRONT TO THE BACK OF THE BUS

From quaaludes in middle school, I turned to the weed. I spluttered and coughed, unable to inhale, but I was determined to have that buzz, so I kept trying. I soon graduated to alcohol, which became my drug of choice because it was so easy to get. It was a steady progression to blackout drunkenness most nights of the week. My friends and I would sneak bottles of Jack Daniels from our parents' liquor cabinets or buy drinks with our fake IDs from the drive-through bars that proliferated between the two coasts of northern and central Florida.

When I showed up for class, it was for the "social hour," as one of my teachers complained, not learning. The rest of the time I skipped school altogether, strung out on whatever with my friends and playing music by the bleachers: "Carry On Wayward Son" by Kansas, "Another Brick in the Wall" by Pink Floyd, "(Don't Fear) The Reaper" by Blue Oyster Cult . . . The experimentation continued with LSD, acid, crystal meth, and whatever else I could get my hands on that didn't involve piercing my skin with a needle. In no time I migrated from the front to the middle to the back of the bus. (Heather had long since migrated to the Mustang her parents gave her.) My grades slid from mediocre to failing as I skipped more classes. Before long I was a teenage addict, and out of control.

So why, in a book about leadership, am I sharing these details of my messed-up formative years? Why would the story of my addiction, my journey to rock-bottom, be educational to anyone running a business or aspiring to lead? Because it shows that *anyone* can rise. Every single human being has potential buried within, and it's important to recognize that fact in yourself as well as others. It's just that sometimes it's buried under so many layers and years of dysfunction, misfortune, mental illness, and tragedy that it can take a while to find it. But stick with me because I'm going to show you exactly how to dig deep and get there.

Had I not, I could easily have become a statistic. Addiction was in my DNA. My mother, a strikingly beautiful half-Cherokee woman with long black hair that hung like silk curtains down her back, was a raging alcoholic. So was her father, and most likely his father before him. My uncle Vernon, Mom's brother, was a Vietnam vet who'd done three tours. After the war he came back to his family, already lost in the throes of alcoholism. He was so haunted by the war that he used to mutter to himself in Vietnamese, *"Di di mau! Di di mau!"* (Go away! Go away!)—something he and his fellow combatants used to shout at the enemy. Uncle Vernon was doing his best just to stay alive but died too soon from cirrhosis of the liver.

My mom was a deeply troubled soul. Like many addicts, she suffered from mental illness, although in those days a diagnosis was rare. If I had to guess it was somewhere far up on the spectrum of bipolar disorder, and she drank as a way of coping. But instead of taking the edge off her moods, the booze made her rage. Thank God for my grandmother, who somehow managed to skip the addict gene and never touched alcohol. A Baptist church lady, she was always there for us with a homecooked meal or a freshly baked pie, filling some of the maternal void. My grandfather passed, but the story was that he was extremely violent toward his wife and kids. With him gone, Grandma was free to focus all her love and attention on her grandchildren, taking turns between Mom and my uncle Vernon's house.

FIRE WATER

We never really discussed it, but I know my mother suffered her own childhood traumas and never managed to break the cycle of abuse. Sabrina and Kim remember much more than I do, because

I was probably no more than five years old at the time. Being the baby protected me from some of the worst abuses. For that reason my sisters carry a lot more pain. They reminded me how we used to all hide together in one of our bedrooms at night when the adults in the family were angry and intoxicated.

Mom became especially volatile when she was drunk. The fire water brought the fire out. Yet, in her sober moments, she could also incredibly loving and fiercely protective. In second grade one of my teachers wore a big class ring. He turned it inside his hand, then smacked me on top of my head, along with all the other kids in my class. My mother could not understand why I kept coming home from school with headaches. When I explained what was happening, she called my stepdad, a former cop, then put on every ring she had, hopped in her Pontiac Trans Am, and drove over to the school.

Heads turned as this stunning woman walked in, all legs in her miniskirt, looking like a Native American warrior going into battle. She made her way toward homeroom, where my teacher still sat grading papers. Meanwhile, about four or five police cars pulled up outside as backup for Mom, courtesy of her husband's connections.

"How you would like me to lay this hand on *your* head?" she asked my teacher, holding up a hand so full of metal her rings looked like a knuckle duster.

My teacher looked terrified, as he should have been, while the school principal stood off to the side, mortified. Mom's point was made. She got me moved from his class, and I never had to deal with him again. As I recall, my teacher also stopped laying his hands on the other kids' heads. As far as Mom was concerned, no one could touch her kids. Except her.

When you lead people, it's important to understand the human condition and realize that no one is *all* good or *all* bad. Human beings are complex creatures filled with brilliance, darkness, and shadows. With the right guidance, they can be brought into the light—they can become the best version of themselves—but not everyone gets that nurturing when they need it most. Millions of people are born into generations-long cycles of abuse they have not been able to break, and Mom was one of them.

She smothered us with love, and cruelty, like Jacqueline and Hyde. There wasn't much middle ground with her. On our better days we were a loving, hugging family. We had cookouts in the yard every weekend. Then her dark side would take over, even more so after my father left when I was eight years old. At that point Mom had to go to work to provide for me and my two sisters and took a job waitressing. It wasn't long before she caught the eye of my stepdad, who owned a working ranch just outside of Bradenton, a few miles inland from Florida's west coast.

DOWN ON THE FARM

Things were good for a while. My mother had extended periods of calm because she was happy in her new marriage. We kept ourselves busy outdoors, tending to the livestock, riding horses, and doing shifts in the meat shop my stepdad Bill had on the property. A typical day would include getting up with the roosters, feeding the animals, going to school, doing our homework, feeding the animals again, cleaning out the stables, and all the other chores that go along with living on a working farm. Bill also had a massive meat warehouse. He taught us how to butcher the pigs and cows, wrap them, and store them. We were basically his slave labor, but I kind of loved it, especially the part where I got to take care of the animals.

When I was eight my science teacher (not "Mister Smackhead") decided to stop by the ranch and see for himself what my life was like, because he didn't exactly believe me when I told him I woke up at the crack of dawn to do chores hours before first period at school. During hay season we were especially busy. Bill, along with our stepbrother Lamar, my sisters Kim and Sabrina, and me, drove his truck 10 miles to a farm to gather hay to bring back to our barn for animal feed. We had a gooseneck trailer on the back. Kim, who was the littlest, drove the truck slowly alongside the bales, using a block of wood to help her reach the gas pedal. The rest of us ran alongside, grabbing stacks and passing them up to Bill, who stood on the flatbed stacking them neatly. It was backbreaking work.

My teacher wanted to see for himself why I was so exhausted by the middle of the afternoon, so he followed me around as I did my daily chores. When he watched me counting out someone's change in the store, witnessed my customer service skills, and realized the full extent of the business operation and my responsibilities on our farm, he told my parents:

"This is giving Sandy a better education and work ethic than anything I could teach her in a classroom."

If only my old teacher could have written my resume! When you are building or choosing your path in a particular business or industry, try to look back on the totality of your experience, and not just what ticks the conventional career box. See yourself through the eyes of a supportive teacher, friend, or family member. And, when you're the one doing the hiring, you'd be wise to do the same, because the best predictor of someone's work ethic isn't necessarily a degree from Harvard or an internship at McKinsey, however impressive those credentials may be.

I was one of those kids who could never sit still and would have chosen hard labor over doing nothing every time. When our work was done, we were rewarded with playtime on the lake. We rode motorboats, water-skied, and used Jet Skis. On land we rode horses, raced dirt bikes, mini motorbikes, and ATVs. It was always competitive, which I loved. It was hard-earned fun. My stepdad encouraged us to do it all the right way, taking care of all the equipment and treating the environment with respect, whether on water or the land. It was the same with horses. Sometimes we'd ride on horseback about 20 miles to an equestrian arena to participate in barrel races (this was before I-75 was built, so horses were a great way to get around). As soon as we got back home those horses had to be fed, watered, and groomed, and their stables mucked out. But I did those chores gladly, and with a kind of reverence.

So, that's what was going on in my life when I popped my first pill. In that moment, my life seemed okay. I've always been one to focus on the good moments, and there was plenty of light to relieve the darkness. At home I was never bored, and I don't recall feeling depressed exactly, so I don't necessarily see a direct causal link between my addiction and our family's dysfunction. It was peer pressure mostly, a desire for acceptance and to do what everyone else was doing. To a lesser extent, it may have also been a way of dealing with my sexuality, although the fact of my being gay was never something at the front of my mind.

I knew that I was attracted to other girls from the time of my first crush in kindergarten. There was this one cutie with long curly hair who I hugged and held hands with, pouring all the affection in my five-year-old being onto her. Of course it was innocent, but there was no doubt that my feelings were romantic, and that I was the prince to her princess. There were other crushes, and a few fumbling make-out sessions with girls and boys during my teen years. It was not something you'd dare give voice to back then, in the '70s, '80s or even the '90s, especially growing up in small town Florida in a strict Baptist family.

So, for the most part, I compartmentalized my sexuality and shoved it into the back of my mind. By then I was much more interested in getting wasted than getting laid anyway. Diving deep into who I was and coming to terms with my sexuality was way down on my to-do list. Michelle thinks it was part of the reason for my addiction, but I'm not so sure. When you are an addict there is nothing else in life, not even sex, and much less love.

OUR OWN FUN

So much of my youth was spent in a fog. Throughout my addiction I was arrested 14 times, mostly for DUIs and/or driving without a license. After my tenth arrest, Mom and my stepdad declared me "ungovernable" to the court and sent me to live with my father, who had by then moved halfway across the state to Dundee, a small town in Central Florida. It was such an acrimonious divorce that I hadn't seen much of my dad since I was seven years old. Suddenly I had a new family, including my stepmom, Shirley, two stepbrothers, and a stepsister—Beau, Mark, and Michelle, although Beau was older and mostly out of the house by then. It was a quiet, suburban home with strict but loving parents, and where life was peaceful and wholesome until I came along. Dad, who was a welder by trade, had done well in his new life. He even saved up enough to buy a truck to haul asphalt. He worked long, hard hours to create a comfortable, middle-class life for us all. His wife, the ultimate homemaker, sewed clothes, cooked, and cared for us.

I don't even like to use the term "step" because Dad's family by marriage quickly became *my* family. Michelle, who is less than a year younger than me, was closest to me in age, and we grew closer in many ways than I am to my sisters by birth. We bunked in the same room and shared everything, talking late into the night. We played together, always doing something outside, dancing to music on the portable stereo, playing racquetball and tennis in the street outside our house. My childhood predated the digital age, so we made our own, physical fun. Sometimes I took it a little too far, like when Michelle and I raced down a hill on our bikes. I was so hellbent on winning I clipped the front of my sister's bike and went flying, giving myself a terrible road rash from crash-landing on the pavement. When the doctor tried to scrub out the gravel I ran screaming out of his office. It wasn't the first or last of many hard falls.

Our fridge was always well-stocked. It was that kind of home. We got enough pocket money to buy ourselves a chocolate milkshake from the Dairy Queen, and Shirley (whom I called "Mom") always made sure there was plenty of fresh ground beef so we could make ourselves burgers for our after-school snack. We made doughnuts in the deep fryer, then burned off the calories running around the neighborhood until dusk, when it was time to get back for the family dinner. The rule was we had to be home by the time the streetlights came on. Then we did the dishes, watched a little TV, and turned in by 10 p.m. on school nights—or at least that's what was expected.

THE OPPOSITE OF ME

Michelle had no problem following those rules. She was that child who never did any wrong. She did her homework, never backtalked to our parents, and got straight A's in school. She was the total opposite of me—focused and goal-oriented, the *yin* to my *yang*. Even today, I call her my second brain. She remembers so much from the past that I can't recall. She's also a logical, linear thinker, with a fresh and brutally honest perspective—feedback that helps me to round out some of my most important decision-making. Who doesn't need a sister who isn't afraid to tell you the truth?

As different as we were, Michelle also came from a broken home, except that it was her father who was the abusive alcoholic. My dad brought the stability to her life she craved.

"Tell me the truth: Am I the milkman's daughter?" Michelle still jokingly asks her mother, because she's the only one in our blended families who did not get the addiction gene.

Whatever stage of life and career you are in, surrounding yourself with people who are different from you will only strengthen your leadership skills. As I write this, corporations are hot on the topic of diversity, equity, and inclusion (DEI). It's a major priority for businesses to ensure that enough minorities and people representing different abilities, genders, as well as the LGBTQ communities are being hired not just at the entry level or mid-management positions but for top positions.

DEI initiatives are the right thing to do. They move the needle forward in business because they bring a broader range of experiences and perspectives to the table, which can ultimately lead to better decision-making. It exposes you to other possibilities you might not have considered. Michelle was the one Girl Scout in my circle of hippies and dropouts. Now I am not saying she necessarily led me to make better decisions growing up, but my exposure to her clean-cut, rules-following way of being must have planted a seed that laid dormant for years.

Of course, I tried my best to corrupt her, including getting her to smoke a cigarette. I wanted her to loosen up and join me in being naughty now and then. Our parents caught us and made us eat and inhale a whole pack, so that was the first and last time for Michelle. She never got on that merry-go-round with me. Instead of allowing me to be a bad influence on her, she was more like the older sister even though she was younger, doing all she could to be a good influence on me. It never worked. By the time we became bunkmates I was already deep into my addiction.

"Sandy, noooo!" she always pleaded with me when I snuck out through our bedroom window after our parents had gone to bed. "You'll get in trouble!"

DEI initiatives are the right thing to do. They move the needle forward in business because they bring a broader range of experiences and perspectives to the table, which can ultimately lead to better decision-making. It exposes you to other possibilities you might not have considered.

Michelle's efforts were futile because I chose trouble every time. But she accepted me for who I was and did her best to cover for me with our anxious parents. One night, when I was 15, I stole Shirley's car, sneaking it out of the driveway by putting it in neutral and pushing it. But in my inebriated state I called the house at 3 a.m. when I meant to call a friend. Woken out of a dead sleep, Michelle picked up, assuming I was home and asleep in the bunk above her. By then the ringing of the phone, back when landlines sounded like fire alarms, had woken up the whole house. Everyone was startled, confused, and afraid something had happened to me. Shirley woke up next, checked the driveway, and saw the car was missing. In my inebriated brain I knew I was busted. I rolled it back into the driveway and walked into the house, scared.

My dad was furious and told me I had to go back to live with my mom. Bouncing between my mom and dad's house, getting kicked out because I was too much to handle—it was a vicious cycle. My parents did their best with what they had to work with, but I guess I presented quite the challenge for any parent.

Shirley once found a bottle of Jack Daniels I hid behind the house. "Is this yours?" she asked me, knowing full well it was, because she never touched the stuff and my father hardly drank. They kept liquor for company, but I don't think I ever saw Dad sip more than one beer a year.

"Nope!" I answered.

She asked me again and I stuck with my answer.

"I know it's yours," she insisted.

"Are you sure?" I replied, in full denial, not because I was being cute. I truly did not remember putting the bottle there. Then again, who else's could it have been?

THROUGH THE FOG

Few moments stand out for me during that period of my life from the age of 13 until I finally got sober at 25. I was in a state of almost uninterrupted oblivion. I smoked pot every day. My friends and I played quarters, and I "won" every time. I remember once laughing uncontrollably and hysterically the time I dropped acid. But it wasn't mirthful laughter. Having such an intense, volatile reaction was overwhelming, even painful. My sides ached the next day from the laughter convulsions. I also remember doing crystal meth for the first time and walking around our high school football field with a friend.

"These hills are really hard to walk up," I said, believing I was hiking up a mountain.

"Sandy, this is not a hill," my friend, who was dealing with her own hallucinations, informed me.

The more drugs I experimented with, the more I craved them. By the time I was 17, after more than one arrest, a judge ordered me to go into treatment. There I was, a young kid in a rehab facility with people from all walks of life, from skid row to executives, watching people go through withdrawal and suffer terrifying hallucinations. Seeing someone experience delirium tremens, or DTs—sweating, shaking, and shrieking at their imaginary monsters—is beyond disturbing.

When you first entered the facility, staff would take you into the bathroom and make you drop your pants. I watched as people tried to sneak their fixes in all kinds of strange places. I got to see what addiction did to people at its most advanced stages, physically and mentally. But I was young and cocky. *I'll never get that bad*, I told myself.

I had a revolving door to my local treatment center. By the time I turned 20, I had learned well how to manipulate the system. With every arrest I told the judge I was an addict, because rehab was much more pleasant than jail despite the strung-out inmates. And I knew the recovery lingo so well that I could convince whoever was assessing me that I was on the right path and ready to go out into the world again.

Like other addicts, I'd become a bottom feeder—one of those sea creatures that suck up whatever they can from the bottom of the sea floor. Those squid, bass, and bivalves are laser-focused on their quest for algae and plant life to sustain them, and not much else. But at least they're part of a natural cycle. Addicts are not. Instead of putting something back into the world, I was constantly taking, because, when you're not sober, that's what you do. I bounced around between Dad's house in Dundee; friends' couches in Bradenton where the booze, drugs, and parties were plentiful; and my mom's and grandmother's homes in Bradenton. Grandma never refused me when I asked to "borrow" some cash. I had places to sleep and meals for free, and because I didn't have to pay my own bills I could focus my attention on scoring that next bottle of tequila.

RAYS OF LIGHT

But some of the lessons I learned through recovery began to sink in slowly, like a rare beam of sunshine from the surface of the sea that reaches down, fathoms deep, and pierces through the murk. One of the first things I learned as I was faking my way through recovery was that I needed to find a job, any job, no matter how humble, and make a point of showing up for it every day. At 17, I started cleaning boats around the marina in Bradenton. It was casual employment. I wasn't on a payroll or anything. Yet there was no shortage of this type of work, and in recovery one of the first things they tell you to do is find a job, anything, even if that means digging ditches or waitressing at Denny's, which I tried and lasted all of a day. I was kicked out of high school by grade 11, so it wasn't like I had a lot of options on the work front.

During one of my sober periods, I found work in a boat parts factory, then lost the job six months later when I started drinking again. But I kept coming back to cleaning boats. Having grown up by the ocean, I loved being on the water. It felt like home, and the physicality of the work suited me. It didn't matter that I was starting literally at the bottom, scraping off algae and barnacles, cleaning out the bilges and hosing down sludge, oil, and dirt. Keeping boats clean from the hull to the motor maintains their value and keeps them running safely. Looking after something that carries you safely across the water and brings so much joy is part of the deal in boating, in the same way you would brush down your horse after a good, long gallop. I took pride in the smallest details of my handi-work. I got to be outside, and I could see the results of my labor, so it planted another small seed of motivation.

Cycling in and out of recovery, certain moments stuck with me, like the letter I wrote to my father. It was 1987, I'd just turned 23, and I was back at another alcohol treatment center. As part of the process of letting go of past hurts, the counselors made us write letters to the people who shaped our lives: our siblings, our parents. You put everything in writing—all the dark corners of your memory bank. There is something about the act of physically writing it down that gives those feelings shape, so that they can be dealt with some-how. You leave nothing unsaid, so that you can release all those feelings and forgive.

Mine was an angry letter. Until I put pen to paper, I had no idea there was so much sadness and bitterness inside me. After years of being numb and feeling hopeless, emotions I didn't even know I had welled up inside me, and I really let Dad have it.

"You left us," I wrote. "You abandoned us! What kind of father leaves his kids? You were our daddy. But you didn't care!"

I gave the whole story of being left to fend for ourselves with our deeply troubled, alcoholic mother. Then I read my letter to the group of other addicts who were with me in counseling. Everyone was sobbing but me. I still felt nothing.

Next, I had to read the letter to my father. I had to sit across from him and make him receive all my anger, hurt, and shame. He took it like the man he was. And then it was his turn.

There were so many things I hadn't known about our family's history. As a child, all I heard was Mom's side of the story. When I was four, Dad had almost died from kidney cancer. He was weak from the chemo treatment, but he still had to contend with my mother's addiction, which got so bad he had to hunt through the house for hidden bottles of liquor, and even found a stash in the toilet tank! A mostly gentle guy, at least toward me, who rarely drank, he'd reached a point where he could no longer deal with her addiction. Their fights were epic as she cycled in and out of sobriety. She hit him too.

"It was die or survive," he told me (remember, Mom had a shotgun). "I love you girls; I fought for you."

I had no idea Dad tried to get custody. When I finally understood the love that had been there all along, I broke down in tears. All was forgiven.

In fact, after years on the couch, speaking with one therapist after the next, I forgave everyone. I never wanted to hold on to the bitterness of the past, hence my selective memory. I always felt my family's love, despite the extreme dysfunction. All those factors that lead to my addiction: being born into a family that had suffered abuse and addiction for generations, the aftershock of the divorce, being shipped across the state to become my father's problem, the desire for acceptance, the raging hormones of puberty, the dim awareness of being different sexually, even the ADHD, were factors that went into the circumstantial soup that put me on that self-destructive path. It's the same when you're navigating the sea. It's often a confluence of conditions that create the hazards and throw your boat off course. But I was slowly beginning to understand, accept, and let go. I was transitioning from unthinking and impulsive, to conscious and self-aware.

HARD-HEADED

But my addiction wasn't over yet. I started drinking again. I would do the work of recovery, stop, then start again. It still hadn't quite hit me that I had a choice. It was up to me to make that decision every day not to abuse alcohol or drugs, but I still had to ask for help and do the work. I had to turn my will over to a power greater than myself. And I guess I hadn't yet forgiven the last person in my world I needed to forgive—myself.

With the benefit of hindsight, I can see how brutal it must have been for Michelle, my father, Sabrina, Kim, and all the other family members and friends who cared about me to see me hit bottom, then go into recovery again and again, never quite knowing if it would stick. They wondered if I would keep trying or sink even deeper, winding up dead. My last DUI, when I was 23, I came close.

I was racing through the streets of Bradenton in my car, so completely out of it that I crashed into a parked car. Always a fan of speed, I must have been going at least 80 miles an hour because my head went through the windshield and shattered the glass on impact. Apparently, my eyelashes were stuck to the glass. I felt the warmth of blood gushing down my face before I lost consciousness, but that's all I remember from the experience. The paramedics found a vial of cocaine on the floor of the vehicle and assumed the crash was a result of my hunting around for it, but I couldn't say for sure whether that's what really happened.

My family was shaken. I'd had drunk-driving accidents before, but nothing like this. I nearly lost my left eye, and I still have a scar from where a shard of glass sliced through my eyelid and browbone; I had to stay in the hospital for several days. Sabrina was with me, squeezing my hand because they couldn't administer pain medication while I was still high. She threw up when she witnessed the ER doctor go into my eye socket to sew up the tear, which involved pulling the skin of my eyelid through the hole.

But it could have been so much worse. I was lucky my head is so hard!

By no means am I suggesting I deserve a cookie for any of this. I own my past, the people I hurt, and the mistakes I made. But the larger point for business leaders to understand is that there's value in those who've climbed back up from failure. Perseverance is priceless. When you're at the height of a wave, it's easy. You're at the top, surfing, feeling that sense of elation as you ride it down. But then you hit the trough at the bottom. That's where character has to shine. The real work is getting back up and repeating, keeping that same positive mentality while never allowing the undercurrent to suck you back in.

It would be two more years before I got clean and stayed clean. But this time I was trying. I tried and failed and tried again. That's the thing about recovery. There is no magic bullet. Addiction is not something that you can just solve. Like diabetes, there is no cure because it's always with you. The "medication" so to speak happens day by day, step by step, and, yeah, sometimes you stumble. Every day you must decide. *Are you going to get back up? Will you go to a meeting? Is today the day you show up, give back, and put something positive into the world?*

GOD FIRST

I am sharing my recovery journey with you because it demonstrates how anyone can get back up from the bottom. Whether it's sex, drugs, alcohol, or gambling, millions of people have an addiction disorder that masks an untreated mental illness. At least 10 percent of the adult population in the U.S. is dealing with drug addiction, and the numbers are growing fast. But, when you make that decision, when you discover that sense of purpose and the will to fulfill it, it doesn't matter if you flunked out of high school. Who you know, where you're from, even how much money you have in your bank account doesn't matter. The only thing that does matter is that you are putting in the work.

Wake up, say a prayer, brush your teeth, make your bed, get dressed, go to work, go to a meeting, come home, say another prayer, and go to bed. That was my routine. You'd be surprised. Some people can't even bring themselves to take a shower. But it starts with something that small—a commitment to self-care at its most basic. (Today, for me, it's exercise first thing in the morning. For others it might be yoga or a meditation session.)

Next, you show up for the humblest of jobs, whether that's washing dishes or swabbing decks, because you need gainful employment. In doing so day in and day out, you learn about structure and consistency. They say it takes 30 days to build a habit. You get into a groove, so that when you do slide back you know the simple and small steps you need to take to get back into it, like washing your hair or punching the clock. You create the foundation necessary to become a productive member of society.

Would I have hired me while I was in the throes of my addiction? Of course not! But one of biggest takeaways I want to give business leaders reading this book is that, once they've gone through the process of recovery and shown some consistency in doing the work, once they are sober and have shown that they can remain so, those who've gone through it can be among the most dedicated employees on your payroll. I've heard from thousands of people who've gotten clean and are seeking that lifeline. They'd do anything for a chance to be useful, have a purpose, and build a career. They'll work harder than anybody and become your greatest assets.

Until I got sober, I was in and out of various county jails and institutions. I was a burden to the taxpayer, and I was giving nothing back. So earning a paycheck, no matter how small, was transformational. I became a taxpayer; I had a stake in society. But it was more than that. I was slowly learning that I had to give myself over to God's will. Growing up, we went to church, but I hadn't necessarily internalized its spiritual teachings. But the fellowship that comes with recovery and sobriety reminds you that you are part of something bigger. My purpose was to give back.

In 2015, Denzel Washington gave a commencement speech to Dillard University that has become one of my mantras: "God First."

He talked about how he was sitting in his mom's hair salon on March 27, 1975, wondering what he was going to do with his life as he was flunking out of college with a 1.7 grade point average. An old woman peeked out from under the hair dryer and made a prophecy that he would travel the world and speak to millions of people. But that fact that she was so accurate about his success wasn't the lesson.

"I've been protected. I've been directed. I've been corrected. I've kept God in my life, and it's kept me humble. I didn't always stick with him, but he always stuck with me. So stick with him in everything you do."

Oh, and Denzel added one more piece of advice at the end of this speech. He told the graduates to shove their slippers under the bed, so that when you roll out of bed you need to go down on your knees to find them, and while you're there, you pray.

ON YOUR KNEES

That speech reminded me of a conversation I had with my first sponsor, Terry, a beautiful, brassy Boston big mouth. She impressed my 17-year-old self because of the nice car she drove and the cool music she played. She represented everything I wanted in life. She was who I wanted to become. And, boy, was she tough! When I called her to complain about my life and make excuses for myself, she refused to coddle me.

"Sandy, did you get on your knees and pray this morning?"

"Well, no."

"Did you go to a meeting?"

"Yeah."

"Oh really? And did you pay attention, serve as a greeter, stay afterward to help out, or do anything service oriented, or did you just sit and drink the free coffee?"

"Um, the latter?"

"Okay, Sandy, go to bed because the day is over. Do all those things tomorrow, *then* call me and tell me how you feel."

I'd been repeating the same actions, or inactions, and expecting different results. But I was finally reaching that point where I truly did want to do all the above. I wanted to stay clean and contribute something to the world. The DUI arrests, the broken bones, cuts and bruises, the sadness in the eyes of the people who loved me . . . it was getting old.

In 1987, after the car accident, I moved to Fort Lauderdale, where I got treatment at Stepping Stones, which is what's known as a three-quarter house, where you're considered more or less independent after completing a halfway house program. By answering an ad in the paper I found full-time employment in the industry I loved, detailing and maintaining some of the finest yachts on Florida's East Coast. I was good at my job. It felt gratifying when clients showed their appreciation for the quality of my work. Truly earning that paycheck bolstered my self-confidence. After completing my program in Stepping Stones, I was given the chance to crew on my first boat. After going to sea, I had the opportunity to observe some of the operational aspects of a charter. I was learning and growing in a field I would never have known existed if I hadn't stumbled onto it.

I started seeing myself succeeding in the maritime world and imagining how far it could take me. At one point, I decided to become a dive instructor. Getting the training and licensing helped me prove to myself that I was capable of learning and becoming qualified to do more than just grunt work. But boats kept calling to me.

Two years later, in 1989, I got sober for good. There was nothing dramatic about it this time. There was no car accident or face-plant on a sidewalk to force my hand. I just woke up one morning after a drug-induced night and no longer felt a desire to repeat that feeling. I still had my car. It wasn't lost or impounded like it had been in the past. I had money in the bank, so this time I had something to lose.

I was simply ready. For the first time in my life, I felt a greater desire to stay clean than to get high. Something inside me had finally shifted. I broke through to the surface of the sea where I've remained, breathing the bracing salt air ever since.

- **You have a choice.** There are countless reasons why someone can fall into addiction. It's a disease that's often the result of some untreated mental illness. But even if it's in your family's DNA, addiction doesn't have to be your fate. I am not my mother. You can choose unhealthy coping mechanisms such as booze, narcotics, weed, gambling, sex. . . . Or healthy strategies such as exercise, talk therapy, giving back, prayer. . . . The decision is yours to make, every day.

- **Create healthy habits.** Get up, brush your teeth, make your bed, go to work, do something good for somebody else, repeat. Whether you're in recovery or just trying to maintain a positive and productive headspace, practice some simple, accessible life habits you can always come back to when you find yourself spiraling. Even if the day is half over, you can still begin again. Start your day over in your mind. You can also hit the gym, get pumped with an inspiring song (or calm down with a soothing song), say something encouraging to someone else, pray. There's always time for a reset. I often repeat to myself this little rhyme: "I feel good, I feel fine, I feel like this all the time."

- **Stop thinking about "me" and start giving back.**
  You can't find happiness if you go through life
  always thinking about your own wants and desires.
  Help another person in need, not with your money
  but with your time. Pause to listen to someone else.
  The gift of giving is that you will no longer be in
  the mindset you were in before you helped another
  person. The greatest gift is to give something back
  into the world, whether inspiring others or working
  hard and doing the next right thing. But only you
  know what that is for you.

- **Include people in your circle who think differently
  from you.** Once you've brought in those different
  perspectives, chances are you will make better
  decisions.

- **Understand the power of second chances.** Leaders,
  you'll never find a more dedicated team member than
  someone who has come out the other side of extreme
  hardship or fought the good fight of recovery.

- **Put God, or whatever you see as a power greater
  than yourself, first.** It's not all about what *you* want.
  Recognize that you are a part of something bigger
  and allow yourself to receive. In these next chapters,
  I'm going to share many moments when God's will
  overruled my own, and the outcomes were so much
  better than anything I could have dreamed up for
  myself. As Denzel said: "Everything that you think
  you see in me. Everything that I've accomplished.
  Everything that you think I have—and I have a few
  things. Everything that I have is by the grace of God."

- **You've got this.** If I can make it from where I was as
  a teenage addict to where I am now as a superyacht
  captain with a hit TV series, there is absolutely no
  reason why you can't raise yourself to heights you

never dreamed for yourself. Yes, we experienced a tough couple of years with a global pandemic, economic hardship, and isolation. More people are suffering from addiction as a result. But if you put in the work, there's nowhere to go but up.

Chapter 3

CAPTAIN OF
MY SOUL

*If one does not know to which port one is
sailing, no wind is favorable.*

—SENECA

The water was getting choppy in Fort Lauderdale's Marriott Marina, which was home base for many of Florida's superyacht owners, including my new boss, John Flynn. He'd just slipped his 67-foot Hatteras into position, and he wanted me to dock his 38-foot Cigarette Top Gun boat right next to it. If you haven't seen one of these things race around the coastal waters, you'd probably recognize the type from the old James Bond movies, or in *2 Fast 2 Furious*. Back in those days, that vessel would have cost about $250,000. It was bobbing in the water like a kid's toy, yet I had to somehow dock this vessel alongside his Hatteras without doing any damage to its hull. There was zero room for error. I felt nauseous.

After my fifth turn, John screamed down from the bow of the yacht, "Sandy, just dock the damn boat!"

So I docked the boat.

In all his gruffness, John knew that I was stuck in my fear. He understood that the only way to get me out of my head was to give me no alternative but to do it, to jolt me into action. When it was no longer up to me, when he was barking an order and I no longer had the luxury to overthink, muscle memory took over.

It was one of many leadership lessons I learned from this wily and occasionally gruff businessman who eventually became like a second father to me. John's operational knowledge of boating, as well as his extensive experience as a successful business entrepreneur, became my early foundation as a captain. At that period of my life I could not have found a better mentor. By no means was he a soft touch. Empowering someone is never to be confused with enabling. But he gave me a sense of agency, allowing me to learn by doing while remaining close by in case I needed further instruction.

He was hands on just enough, like a human set of training wheels, shadowing me until he believed I had it down cold. Once he did, he would go down to the aft deck to join the clients he was entertaining, pour himself a glass of White Star champagne, never giving it a second thought as I navigated his boat down through the Florida Keys, or Harbor Island in the Bahamas, or north to Charleston, South Carolina, and all the way back up to his hometown of Boston. He pointed me in a direction, and I just went, but much farther than I ever thought I could go. Meeting this man opened up a world for me that I never knew existed.

CIRCLE OF SOBRIETY

I'd already established a circle of sober friends in my personal life—a crew of fellow travelers who believed in me. Their encouragement was crucial to my recovery. They held me accountable and continually reminded me that I was worthy and capable. My sober friends were like family.

But there wasn't an individual in the maritime industry who knew my past and saw my full potential the way John did. At that point I only had a vague sense of what I wanted to do in the boating world. I didn't even know what was possible, or the steps it would take to focus my ambition and turn it into something real. John came along at just the right time and place to be that person who raised the bar for me, encouraging me to reach for specific goals with a not-always-so-gentle nudge.

I was two years sober by then. The period between 1989 and 1991, when I started working for John, my work ethic had supercharged.

There was something about starting my life as an adult at 25 that made me feel I had to make up for lost time, so I gave my all to every task, however menial. (Leaders, that's the power of second chances.)

While at Stepping Stones—the sobriety house where I lived with 42 other women—I found work at a nearby meat processing company. It was a flashback to my childhood working on my stepdad's ranch, including the crazy hours. Every morning I got up before the sun and took a public bus to the factory. It was the first time in my life I'd ever taken public transportation. I punched in at 4 a.m. and out at 3 p.m. The routine was brutal, but it taught me discipline.

After nine months on the meat grind, I saved enough money to pay off my fines and find a place to live. I answered an ad in the paper to crew a yacht based in Newcastle, New Hampshire—a 112-foot Broward. In addition to crewing on the boat, I washed the bottom of it, scraping off barnacles, scrubbing the algae stains, and polishing the stainless steel. I actually enjoyed the grunt work of cleaning teak, scrubbing toilets, and cleaning oil out of bilges. Those of us in recovery always refer to "rust, paint, varnish"—our version of "wax on, wax off" from the movie *The Karate Kid*. Learning a trade from the bottom up was more than gratifying. It felt like redemption. Little did I know that the work I was putting in was also building my character.

But the captain happened to be a raging drunk. Drinking to excess is not uncommon in the boating world, but this guy, who had only one eye, like a pirate, was at the extreme end of anything I've encountered since. He crashed the boat everywhere we went, so we called him "Captain Crunch." He even stole the life rafts off other boats until someone turned him in. The rest of the crew was also deeply dysfunctional. They drank heavily, from morning until night, with no regard for safety, and were reckless with the equipment, cruising in a state of complete chaos. I wanted to learn how to drive the boat, but Captain Crunch didn't let me anywhere near the helm. Watching him, I thought to myself, *I can do better than that!*

I wasn't going to stick around and find out because my sobriety was too new. I needed to protect it by going to meetings, which was difficult to do when we were almost constantly out on the water. Being surrounded by drunkards wasn't exactly helpful, either, although watching that hot mess on water confirmed all the reasons why I didn't want to go back to that life. Waking up every morning fresh and clear felt good. I never wanted that feeling to go away.

But I am grateful for the experience crewing on that Broward because it made clear to me exactly what to avoid if I wanted to continue working with boats. Every situation, even a bad one, is another opportunity to learn. I recognized that my standards of service were on another level from what I'd seen, and that there was an opportunity for me in the maritime industry. It helped me identify a goal, something I could be passionate about, as well as the many thousands of steps it would take to realize my ambition—to become a captain. Whatever it took, at least now I knew I was heading in the right direction.

Every situation, even a bad one,
is another opportunity to learn.

THE BARNACLE BEAT

After that first "experience" crewing and caring for a sizeable vessel, I worked for a boat maintenance company based in Fort Lauderdale called Planned Maintenance. It was the perfect place to land for me, because it enabled me to stay on land, go to meetings, and get acquainted with every inch of some of the most beautiful yachts in the country. I had 14 boats on my route of marinas in the area, where I would pull up in my Jeep, chatting happily to crew members and dockhands as I got out my trusty brush and bucket.

One of my "regulars" was John. The first thing he asked me to do was clean under his engine room, which was a filthy job. The surface was thick with diesel oil and sludge that smelled worse than vomit (and I should know). But I made it gleam. John was never one to heap on praise or express gratitude. In fact, you could work the insides of your hands and fingertips into thick calluses, and he'd still amble over to point out something tiny you may have missed. (That's one thing as a leader I learned not to do from John. You should always encourage your people with praise). Still, I could tell he was impressed. Over the next few weeks, I could also tell he was watching my work, appraising me, my attitude, and my level of dedication.

Over the weeks, John struck up conversations with me. He'd ask me the usual stuff, like where I was from and what I wanted to do with my life. Early on, I shared that I was in recovery, because I'd just received my two-year gold coin from AA, and I was as proud of being two years sober as if I'd just been handed a college degree. At some point in our conversations, I revealed stories of the past I'd left behind—the DUIs, the arrests—and John was unfazed. Far from judging me for my past addiction, he was impressed by my dedication and commitment to sobriety. John was both a pragmatist and an opportunist. It was all about who I was now, and where I saw myself in the future.

"Sandy, how'd you like to come and work for me?" he asked, as I was polishing the stainless steel railings on the aft deck.

I didn't jump at it straight away. I had my own schedule and routine, which gave me plenty of flexibility to go to meetings. Working for John would mean spending a lot of time at sea, and the last thing I wanted was a repeat of my last crewing experience. My priority at that point was to be captain of my own soul more than captain of someone else's vessel; self-leadership before leadership of others.

But I also realized John ran a tight ship. His last captain had left, and his plan was to drive and dock his own boat and have me take care of its daily operations—the more tedious details of boating that were less interesting to him. It would just be me, his then-girlfriend Fran, who would later become his wife, their dog, and the occasional extra crew if necessary.

"I'll teach you everything I know," John promised me. "You'll be my apprentice. I'll even teach you how to drive and dock the boat. You can play with all the toys, travel up and down the coast. We'll go to the Bahamas, the Hamptons, the Caribbean. You will get to see all the best places and mingle with all the best people. If you keep up this level of work, I'll even help you get your captain's license."

It was a real dilemma, because I wanted that job, but my employer in the boat detailing business, Steve Mangini, had been kind to me. Until that point in my life, I'd cheated on everyone who put their faith in me. I was a car thief! Yet Steve was willing to give me a chance. One of the first things they teach you in recovery is how to change a habit. It takes about 30 days of practice. Do the speed limit, not a mile under or over, for a month, and you'll stop speeding. I tried it and it worked. My next challenge was honesty and transparency. These values are the gospel in recovery, one of many life lessons that I'd memorized and internalized, but I needed to be put in a situation that tested my new belief system.

A few hours before I had that conversation with John, someone who was not a client of Steve's asked me to wash his boat.

"Name your price," he said.

I completed the job, then the man wrote out a check and handed it to me. This took place at Gossby's bar on the dock at the Marriott Marina Hotel where Steve was having a drink. He'd observed the whole transaction, although I had no idea I was being watched.

That Friday, I went to Steve's office to collect my paycheck, and I handed him the check I'd been given for that extra job, which I'd had made out to the name of Steve's company, Planned Maintenance. Steve chuckled.

"I must admit I was wondering if you were going to take the money," he said.

"It crossed my mind," I told him. (The old Sandy wouldn't have thought twice about it, but sober Sandy knew better.)

"While we're on the subject, there is something bigger I'd like to discuss with you," I told Steve, filling Steve in on the offer John had just made me and asking him for his blessing.

"I've always wanted to work on one boat, but I know it's a big account. Do you mind?"

"They're a pain in my ass," Steve said. "Go ahead. Take the job!"

It was the first time in my life I'd ever put action to the word "integrity." Who knew that doing the right thing could feel so good? (Investing and taking a chance on someone can yield dividends in terms of loyalty and trust.)

THE INTENTIONAL TASKMASTER

A serial entrepreneur from Boston who bought and flipped boats as both a pastime and an investment (the way some billionaires collect art), John held me to the highest standards. He wasn't a boat captain himself, but he was a hands-on owner who knew his stuff. He was a U.S. Air Force veteran, having served in the aircraft division, and he applied the same system of checks before and after we went out on the water that he used before and after each flight. It was the first thing he taught me.

"Safety is everything," John, a seasoned amateur mariner, told me. "If something goes wrong, you don't want to be out there on the water. We do the engine checks before and after, pre-ignition and post-ignition."

John already knew which mechanisms to test and scan by heart. But they were long checklists, so he had me get everything down in writing first. It was about creating good habits—another element of strong self-development and self-leadership. John's main business was in transportation logistics, and he was methodical and intentional in everything he did on land and sea. Most of his wealth came from leasing out and selling trucks for transporting everything from oil and gas to food for the major supermarket chains around the country. He won huge contracts by convincing these companies that they could operate safely and more efficiently if they replaced their vehicles every four years as opposed to every eight years, for example. He developed proprietary systems that could predict when running these rigs had reached the point of diminishing return in terms of asset depreciation, wear and tear, and maintenance costs. That may be why he liked building his boats new and flipping them after just a few years.

While it's true that some leaders are born, that they have the charisma and "it" factor that inspires others to follow them, the greatest leaders are made. They build on whatever innate gifts they have by learning from others. Whether you're leading a team at a major corporation or running your own business, your success is a result of the sum of your experiences and years of observation. You've studied other leaders, former bosses, or associates to see what they got right, and where they messed up. You've paid attention to understand not just what to do, but what not to do, because no management school on the planet can instill those lessons anywhere near as well as the person who stands before you.

I studied John closely as he nailed down multimillion-dollar deals by wining and dining clients on our indulgent dinner cruises. Why entertain in a restaurant, where they will be distracted and leave when the meal is over? John would take them to his office in Fort Lauderdale, then ply them with his favorite champagne, White Star, dazzling his audience with his mad nautical skills and button-holing some of the key players for his dealmaking on the pretext of stargazing on the bow. Where some entrepreneurs capture clients through quality one-on-one time in a golf cart, John did it where the only means of escaping from him was by jumping overboard. But they were just as captivated by his fact-based persuasiveness. It was masterful!

I had to learn how to hire catering and waitstaff for these high-stakes booze cruises. There was an art to serving well. I came to understand what the expectations were for service and quality for that kind of clientele. Only the best was good enough, but first you need to witness and experience it for yourself. We ate at some of the finest restaurants up and down the Atlantic seaboard. Our summers were spent in New England, based out of Boston Harbor, and in winters we'd do long weekends at Port Lucaya in the Bahamas.

AGAINST THE CURRENT

Port Lucaya has an especially tricky entryway, with shifting channels and treacherous currents. In U.S. ports, someone will go out and proactively dredge the sediment and clear the patch to maintain the depth. But the folks in charge of the ports tend to be more laid back in the Caribbean, allowing tides and the weather to shift the sands to the point where the channel gets shallow and bigger boats can get stuck. Rather than go out and make the channel deeper, these harbormasters are happy to let the next storm move the sand back out again. But John instructed me to take note of previous weather patterns and anticipate where there might be more shallows. He also taught me not to fear them.

"There's a time to be cautious, and there's a time to go for it," John told me. "The worst that can happen is that you kick up some sand. There are bigger dangers, and you have to weigh those with the risk of not taking decisive action."

John started calling me Ace as he put me into increasingly challenging situations. It was a nickname I did my best to live up to, but I had my moments. That first year, we traveled north up the Atlantic coast, and John invited me to take the helm and dock at the North Cove Marina in New York Harbor, by the One World Trade Center. Those waters are crowded and full of crazy currents. This was before I got my captain's license and I didn't feel I had the experience, so I refused. He grabbed the wheel, looked at me, and said, "No guts, no glory." Then he drove against the current. It was another learning moment: it's okay to go against the current. You just have to be willing to push a little harder. (It was why John was a leader I chose to follow, if only out of curiosity.)

When you are completely new to something, there is a tendency to be extra cautious, because your head is full of information about what can go wrong. But John taught me to push past the fear and trust my instincts. It's not a matter of forgetting what you know so much as balancing your knowledge with the bigger picture of what needs to be done, charting your course with the facts in the back of your mind instead of the front, so that you can see exactly where you're going as you forge ahead.

I was on a steep learning curve, about almost everything. When you start your adult life at 25, your reality is a little different and you have a lot of catching up to do. A few months on the job, I pouted because John wanted me to take the boat out on Halloween.

"Sandy, Halloween is not a holiday."

I had my costume all picked out, with plans to trick or treat with my friends (this girl has a sweet tooth), and the big kid in me felt robbed, but I had to grudgingly admit John was right.

FLOATING CORPORATION

Month by month, my responsibilities grew. John called me into his office to learn how to do spreadsheets so that I could track our expenditures and manage our budget, just as a CEO would do in any enterprise. Fran, who was great with computers and data analytics, taught me how to use Microsoft Excel and keep track of the accounts in a professional manner. John never questioned the expenses, but I was still required to track them and stay accountable. I had to provide my boss with quotes from shipyards and understand the services and value each one was offering, to justify the expense. Most yacht owners are lucky if they can break even on their annual operating costs. It was thanks to John's teachings that, a few years later, I was able to run a yacht for First Republic Bank founder Jim Herbert at a tidy profit. *Pure Bliss* cost $780,000 a year to run, but we grossed $860,000 with the charters I booked.

That's another lesson for business leaders. When you assign tasks "above their pay grade" and raise your expectations of the people you lead, they'll jump that much higher to meet them. Giving them a higher goal gives them confidence. If you believe they can do it, then who are they to doubt themselves? And putting that level of faith in someone, or at least seeming to, will seed a deep desire not to disappoint you. You're giving that person the gift of an opportunity to rise.

This details-oriented business training paid off when, a few years later, John entrusted me with supervising his boat builds— massive undertakings where I learned everything about the physical structure of a boat from the hull to the wiring, to intricacies of the engine works. There is nothing like understanding the inner workings of a vessel to develop intimate knowledge of it, knowing exactly how far you can push it, and what it can do for you when you are dealing with rough seas or trying to outrun dangerous weather.

As a boat owner and operator, speed was essential to John. He taught me that it's always better to invest in an engine that's more powerful.

"Sandy, bigger engines are always better," he told me. "Storms don't move much faster than 18 knots, even hurricanes, so if you have a boat that can reach higher speeds, it's worth the cost and fuel consumption to save lives and property."

GOLDEN CHILD

As much as I was John's student in boating and business, we also played together. This man loved his toys. We shared an addiction to fast-moving objects, and during our downtime I'd get to join him as he raced Cigarette boats through the Florida waterways. I suspect he liked having someone who shared his love for speed, which I could indulge in now that I was sober and there were no parked cars for me to crash into. I even coaxed Fran, who was always afraid of getting hurt on one of the water toys, to join us, something she regretted after she slipped off the Hydra-Slide and wound up with whiplash.

Fran used to joke that I was John's golden child, although you'd never guess from his gruff demeanor. But when my father suddenly passed from a heart attack five years after I got sober, John gave me all the paid time off I needed to grieve and spend time with family. (I thank God my father got to see me living a sober life.) John was there for me through it all. Kindness doesn't always show up in words. His compassion took the form of quiet action and constant presence. I was devastated but never felt alone in my grief.

I drew comfort from the new challenges John gave me when I was ready to get back to work. He fulfilled his promise, teaching me all he knew about the mechanics of yachting and navigation, and what he couldn't teach me himself he expected me to figure out and be a self-starter, whether it was washing dishes and serving drinks to well-heeled guests, changing oil and fuel filters, or charting a course through a particularly tricky shipping channel in the Caribbean. He was a big proponent of hands-on learning. Whenever someone gives you that opportunity, seize it! Try out new things while someone more experienced is looking over your shoulder. You can learn so much more by doing.

John was my mentor in an industry where female leaders were and are so rare that at times I feel like a panda. But my gender was of no particular interest to John. He saw the hunger in me to advance and excel in the industry and gave me opportunity after opportunity. He threw me into all kinds of situations so that I could learn by doing. I supervised the builds of his boats, including his 92-foot Hatteras, which he also named *White Star*. On his watch, I also took courses on engineering and maritime law. In 1992, he paid for me to go to the Maritime Professional Training School in Fort Lauderdale to get my 100-ton captain's license.

Whenever someone gives you that opportunity, seize it! Try out new things while someone more experienced is looking over your shoulder. You can learn so much more by doing.

It was an incredible gift that I couldn't squander. At maritime school I was surrounded by people much older than me, tugboat captains who'd been on the water for decades and were finally getting the chance to uprate their qualifications, and it drove home just how fortunate I was, so I hit the books with a profound sense of gratitude.

SETTING COURSE

Even though I flunked out of high school and never acquired the skills to study or ace tests, recovery taught me that I was just as capable as anyone else to learn something by heart. I'd done a lot of reading by then, and as I poured over certain passages of recovery literature over and over again, I was able to memorize lengthy texts. I knew the prayers, even the page numbers they were written on, because I said them out loud every day. I used that same method of repetition as I studied for my captain exams, reading and rereading until I had it down cold.

Another leadership lesson is that, just because you are wired differently, doesn't mean you have any less potential than others to pick up new knowledge or skills. Not all of us are linear thinkers. But what matters is not how we learn, but our *desire* to learn, or what the management consultants are calling "LQ," for learnability quotient. Value the curiosity and willingness to do whatever it takes to adapt, pivot, and grow. In this age of disruption, where processes and technology are constantly changing, we need people who are humble enough to acknowledge what they don't know and curious enough to come at a subject from all sides.

That was me. I had a thirst for knowledge, but my ADHD brain doesn't do well with distractions. (Squirrel!) Knowing my weaknesses as a learner, I created an environment for myself that was conducive to study. To set the right course for my success I put myself in an environment that worked best for me—my local library. I approached my prep work like a regular job, packing a lunch every day and finding my quiet perch at the back of the stacks for eight hours, including a half-hour lunch break, and broke my day up into four periods. In the morning I'd study navigation, charting out various courses in my workbook. I'd study tides and currents, maritime law, and safety. I did this every day for two weeks until I felt competent.

When it was time to take the exam, I traveled to Boston, where the U.S. Coast Guard happened to have availability. I was ready. The test was composed of six sections, with little room for error. If I missed even one question, I could fail. The Coast Guard officer who was monitoring the exam room handed me the test, and there was a question that didn't fall under any of the subject categories I'd prepared for.

"This is not my test," I told the officer.

"Um, yes, it is," he told me. "Please take your seat and answer the questions."

I did as I was told, reading and rereading that final, out-of-the-blue section. *Now why would the maritime school not cover this?* I wondered. *Did they want me to fail? So I went back up to the officer again.*

"Sir, truly, this is not my test. I am sure there's been some mistake."

He checked my registration details and looked at the test again.

"Yes, this *is* your test," he told me.

This went on a couple more times until I realized there was no convincing him. The clock was running out, and I just had to try my best. Shocker, I failed. But I wasn't going to go back to John and tell him he'd wasted his investment in me, because I was completely confident that I'd done the work and was right. Something was off. Livid, I went back to the marine school in Fort Lauderdale to complain.

"That wasn't your test," the academy administrator informed me when I relayed the questions to him.

"Ya think?"

He made a couple of calls and informed me that the Coast Guard had changed the test format the very day I'd taken it, but they failed to communicate this fact to the academy. I was given a private tutor for a week to prepare only for that section I'd missed, then returned to Boston to take the test again. The same Coast Guard officer handed me the papers.

"Is this your test?" he asked me, with a wink.

"This *is* my test," I replied, grinning.

This time, I aced it. My learning challenges and a late start to my adult life could have all become excuses to give up. Instead, after all I'd lived through and survived, I wasn't about to let a minor setback stop me. My sober friends in recovery believed in me. My family believed in me. John believed in me. How dare I not believe in myself?

When you are self-directed and self-aware, when you create the right conditions for yourself to balance out your weaknesses and play to your strengths, you can do anything. That's another example of the power of self-leadership. Your past is irrelevant. You can have total agency to accomplish any goal when you create the right conditions for yourself. Just because I flunked the test the first time didn't mean I was a failure. I simply had to go back and study. If you get pushback, don't take a step back. Do the work and make a comeback!

I became a permanent student of my industry, soaking up every scrap of information that could help me at the helm. If you want to succeed in something, be a student of that career, and always remain teachable. My crew hears me say this often, and you'll read these words more than once on these pages: the learning must be nonstop. Each time I wanted to drive a bigger boat, I needed a new license, and I needed to maintain my existing qualifications with yearly coursework and exams. From the moment I started working on John's boat I was acquiring certifications to advance my career. He didn't tell me it was his plan at the time, but he paid for all of it.

LIKE A LION

Meanwhile, John gave me all the hours I needed captaining his boat to qualify for each additional accreditation. As in the aviation industry, one of the biggest obstacles and expenses for new captains and pilots is getting that time on sea or in the air. Thanks to John, I never had to worry about logging in all those hours. Far from it!

It was reaching the point where I was surpassing my mentor in terms of navigational skills and, I'll just come out and say it, judgment. While sailing into Key West, one of the trickiest locations to dock in U.S. waters, a storm was brewing. All the slips for our sized boat were full. It was like trying to parallel park on a narrow side street in Paris, squeeze into a commuter train in Tokyo at rush hour, or putting on pants while wearing a cast. There was just no way.

That weather blew in like a lion as we were approaching the marina, and I didn't want to try to drive the boat through the narrow entrance with the wind and current. I could see on the radar that it would pass in 30 minutes or so and suggested to John that we wait it out. But he insisted we go in, and I gave him the helm. Once we came into the dock Fran was in a panic state, yelling. As the boat was being blown all over the place, I was zero-focused on getting the vessel secured to the dock as soon as possible.

The Navy doesn't ride storms out in harbors because that's where you can do the most damage. But I had learned over the years with John not to try to change his mind. If he gave me the choice, I would have put our bow to the wind and waited for the storm to pass. And, after about half an hour of whipping rain and chopping waves, it did.

To be fair, weather can throw off even the most experienced navigators. Today there is technology that greatly reduces the margin of error for exactly where and when something is going to hit, although Mother Nature still gets the last word.

In August 1992, just before Hurricane Andrew hit, I flew back from the Bahamas to look after John and Fran's house in Fort Lauderdale. They were headed for Nassau—the heart of "Hurricane Hole"—in the belief that the storm would pass to the north of them. It was always the plan for me to fly home because they wanted some romantic alone time on the boat. John was so relaxed about Andrew, they even told me to leave the wave runners up so they could put them in the water as soon as they got there, which of course I did not. I secured them in the cradle and removed all the other items that could come flying off the vessel.

This was a category 5! Winds got up to 175 miles per hour. It was the worst storm to hit the area in decades. I kept calling John to warn him they were right in its path. John, along with the other boat owners in the marina, agreed to tie the boats together in a spider-web formation. He tied all the boats together, "so it will be all of us or none of us," he later told me. By the middle of the night, John realized he was right in Andrew's path after all. Inch by inch, the storm surge was raising the boats, until the dock lines were just six inches above the pile. Finally, John, Fran, and the other boat crew members and owners decided to get off the water and shelter in a nearby hotel, praying all the while that their spider web would hold. Thankfully, it did, and after a few hours the storm headed north, but not before doing $250 billion worth of damage to the region. Those wave runners would have blown all the way to Bimini if I'd done what I was told.

It had reached a point where John and I were teaching each other. He wasn't always right, but he grew to trust my instincts and listen, which made me more confident in turn. Learning what to do and what not to do from John increased my sense of agency. And when there was something that went beyond his own experience, he continued to invest in my education, like the time he sent me to celestial school so that I could increase my nighttime navigational skills. I was beyond blessed to have found a mentor who believed in me.

It doesn't matter where you are on your journey as a leader, mutual mentorship—the giving and receiving of wisdom—will help you reach that next level. Learn to recognize when someone has something to teach you, and when you have something to teach them. I'll have more to say on mentorship in the following chapters. This two-way street can be with anyone, from anywhere. They can be completely outside of your industry. And when someone has taught you all they can, you remain friends, but you need to recognize that it's time to move on.

NEXT LEVEL

It was as if John had been preparing me to graduate from his own mentorship with each new responsibility. On the business side of boating, John entrusted me to deal with boat brokers and cater to the wealthiest charter clients, including Majid Al Fattaim, the billionaire Arab businessman to whom he sold *White Star* in 2000. This gentleman was so impressed with my knowledge of the vessel that I went with the boat. John hated to lose me, but he realized that, at this next level, I would be navigating in international waters with a brand-new set of challenges that were way beyond anything he could teach me. Until then, I'd only ever run yachts along the coast of Florida and the Caribbean. But in my new role I would be captaining in the Mediterranean as well as the Middle East. After two years, the owner decided sell the 92-foot Hatteras and had me supervise the build of a 157-foot motor yacht: the ill-fated *White Star* of the Red Sea.

It was the first time I had been handed a command of this size. I always believed I could do it. I had this innate understanding of who I could become as a leader. Captaining a boat this size, with close to $100 million under my seat and five or six crew, is like running a company on land, except that, as we learned in Chapter 1, so much more can go wrong on the water. Crews can be unruly, into partying and drinking. Storms can happen. Big waves can knock you sideways. Meanwhile, I am keeping records, managing vendors, doing accounts, and taking care of the owner, who can make demands at the worst possible time as I am trying to get us safely past a swell and into port before nightfall.

It's why I feel so blessed to have been given that solid foundation from John. He set me in exactly the right direction by holding me to the highest standards in terms of operational skills, accountability, and service. My first real job running a boat was just as much an advanced degree in business as it was a crash course in all things related to navigation.

It was also character building. What gave me the poise and calm to get through hell on water in the Red Sea was that solid foundation John helped me build during the previous decade. Before experiencing that high-seas drama I had earned each one of the four gold stripes on my epaulettes. But I also humbled myself to continue my learning, climbing up the ranks, acing all the courses, putting in the hours at sea, and getting my captaining license for every size of vessel, from a 67-foot Hatteras to a 200-foot luxury mega-yacht.

It's possible to lead through a crisis when you've already done the work and acquired the ability. You've put in so much concentrated effort that everything you need is there to tap right under the surface. Time and again, the answers I need and the actions to take just come to me. No need to pause and deliberate. I know exactly what to do and which direction to go.

That confidence and clarity comes from my own personal compass—that gauge for finding my true north that I talked about in Chapter 1. It's about self-leadership. You must always be willing to cultivate self-awareness long after you've earned those stripes if you want to achieve greatness as a leader. Self-leadership requires a deep understanding of your own weaknesses and triggers so that you can manage all those impulses that could lead you down a less productive path. It involves acknowledging and accepting where you are now and the steps you need to take to get to where you want to go. It's the basis of the AA 12-step program that not only saved my life, it gave me the tools I needed to succeed and put myself into a position where I could reach back and bring others forward.

You also need to remain humble and willing to learn from anyone, regardless of rank, in order to own the privilege of influencing and teaching others. John and others reached back to help me, and it's my life's mission to pay it forward. But first I had to believe in myself, finding the internal strength and resources to be rock solid before I could lead others.

As I've learned on the many panels and forums I've attended over the years, leadership, even and especially in the corporate world, requires that you give back or contribute beyond the four walls of your organization, whether that's through mentorship, community outreach, or somehow improving the environment in which you operate. The most successful Fortune 500 CEOs lead with empathy. That's not to say they don't expect accountability or a healthy balance sheet. But we live in a world with so much inequity and existential threats such as pollution and climate change that those of us in positions of power must do something to influence positive change, or at least develop and promote the next generation of leaders who are willing and able, because long-term success won't be sustainable if they don't.

Ultimately, whatever I do in this life must be about something bigger than me. Like the cross currents and interconnectedness of the ocean, we are all connected on a spiritual level, and for that reason we have a deep responsibility to ourselves and our community. We should always strive to have a positive impact through our actions. When I can take a moment to stand in that space, coming from a place of self-love, self-awareness, and self-acceptance, it ripples outward and gently guides my next steps.

- **Surround yourself with positive influences.** And remove yourself from the negative. Yes, you can choose the people who are in your life. I needed to guard my newfound sobriety, but this applies to everyone. If you wish to develop self-leadership, edit out anyone who tries to pull you off your chosen path.

- **Be open to mentorship.** All it takes is one person to believe in you to help you believe in yourself. Stay open because mentors can come from all walks of life. Learn what to do and what not to do, then move on to the next while gratefully acknowledging all that your past teachers and guides have given you.

- **Be a mentor.** Reach back when you've made it to a certain level. Teach the next generation and let them stand on your shoulders.

- **Acquire the skills.** Take the courses, get the hands-on training. Do whatever you can to earn that extra stripe. Even without a benefactor, there are resources out there, from internships to online courses, that will take you forward.

- **Believe in your skills.** Make a quick risk assessment, but do not hesitate. Once you've done the work, trust your own abilities, then attack the problem head on, even if that means driving against the current. Remember: no guts, no glory.

- **Cultivate self-awareness.** Progressing on the course you've charted for yourself requires acknowledging where you are now. Consciously create the right conditions for your own success.

- **Develop self-leadership.** You can't lead others until you've learned the self-discipline to set your own intention and work hard toward a goal. Do all the above, then stand in the confidence of who and what you have become.

- **Remain teachable.** Make a decision about what profession you want to enter or which industry you hope to dominate, then become a permanent student of the field, no matter how far up the ranks you've climbed. Be relentless in your pursuit of learning.

Chapter 4

FATHOMS DEEP

*For our own success to be real, it must contribute
to the success of others.*

—Eleanor Roosevelt

My heart melted for the tiny being wrapped inside his blue and red striped hospital blanket, his limbs wriggling and his huge, long-lashed eyes blinking out the harsh overhead maternity ward lighting. Jessie, my older sister Sabrina's daughter, had just given birth to a beautiful little boy. She tried to stay clean to give her son a great life but relapsed a year later. She asked me to take care of Jeremy until she could get back on her feet, demonstrating the selfless love a mother has for their child.

That very moment I decided to step up. I knew that my niece was deeply troubled, an addict like I had been, and she was in no position to look after herself, much less a newborn. The actual birth father had never been in the picture. We had no idea who, or where, he was. Sabrina, Jeremy's grandmother, was facing her own financial and personal challenges. So I offered to raise Jeremy and co-parent with my partner at the time, Roberta, at least until the day Jessie could get clean and provide for her son herself.

Jessie would always be Jeremy's mother, we made that clear, and she could visit with him whenever she wished. Jessie was clearly in love with her baby boy, so she leaped at the chance to give him a better life than she could give him at that moment. She wanted so much to be with her child, but she understood it was the far better option to keep him with financially and emotionally stable family members rather than risk social services stepping in and putting Jeremy into the foster system.

I'm always going to be there for you little guy, I silently promised him as he gurgled and cooed in his mother's arms. *You will never be drawn down into this life of addiction and dysfunction. Not if I can help it!* I was inspired by the line in the Pink Floyd song "Wish You Were Here" (though I prefer the Melissa Etheridge cover version). "What I wish for you in this lifetime is kindness and to be kind." I call it "Jeremy's song" on my playlist.

So even though I never actually gave birth, that is how I became a parent of sorts. Roberta was very much the "mom" in our unconventional family unit. She raised Jeremy while I provided for him financially. But my career required me to be away at sea for months at a time. When I was on land I was more like the "fun" dad who played, taking him on boat rides and family vacations. I was never the hands-on parent, but I invested in Jeremy as much as I was able to, exposing him to a world of opportunities. Roberta continues to offer him guidance and financial support for his education and career goals. And I am still that person in his life who assures him that he can do anything if he's willing to work for it.

When Roberta and I eventually broke up, we continued to co-parent so that Jeremy could have as much continuity in his life as circumstances would allow. Kim and Sabrina also continued to be presences in his life. Jeremy was surrounded by maternal love. For most of his life, Jeremy lived with my ex, who has been an incredible surrogate parent to our beloved nephew/son. He never lacked for love and attention.

Tragically, Jessie, Jeremy's actual mom, never got sober and passed at 39 years young. Jessie was so like her Aunt Sandy: fun, fearless, and reckless. She was my mini-me, apart from the string of abusive and enabling boyfriends. Our family was always on a knife-edge, worried about what might become of her, but I always had hope that she might make it to the other side of her addiction, which included every kind of substance, from pills to tequila.

There were moments when it looked like she might get clean, but it never took, and, following a diagnosis of pancreatitis, she effectively drank herself to death. Jessie wasn't the only family member whose addiction killed her. A few years earlier, my nephew TJ (Terry Mason Jr.) also lost his life to addiction and, of course, we were devastated. My sisters, Kim and Sabrina, were shattered when their children died. The loss of Jessie hit Jeremy especially hard. I can only pray he will make the right life choices once he digs himself up out of the depths of his grief. But at least I know that Roberta and I did all we could to give Jeremy that solid foundation of love and mentorship.

REACH ONE, TEACH ONE

Whether it's stepping up for a family member or taking the time to write back to those thousands of young people who've shared their struggles with addiction or identity with me and want to know if there is a place for them in my industry, nurturing and inspiring others is what I live for. That, for me, is the whole point of leadership. Every day I aspire to "reach one; teach one," except that being on one of the world's highest-rated reality shows makes it possible to reach millions. It was the whole reason why I agreed to be on *Below Deck Mediterranean* in the first place, because it sure as heck wasn't for the fame and social media craziness! I already had a thriving career. But that success is something I want others to experience too. I firmly believe that investing in individuals, taking a chance on them just as others have invested in me, is what God put me on this earth to do.

Not only is mentoring important in terms of paying it forward and becoming spiritually whole, as a leader it builds intense loyalty in your crew, which is essential in the chartering business, where reputations, safety, and millions of dollars are at stake. By helping others to grow I help to grow myself, my business, and my industry.

Of course, you can only give to those willing to receive. I've always had a sense of who will be most deserving of my investment.

But it's more than just intuition. I observe people closely, noticing their attitude, their enthusiasm for even the smallest of tasks, and the attention they pay to the details. We have conversations and I dive deep into who they are and what motivates them, and I watch closely as they answer. The leaders I admire most are intensely curious about others. They ask questions. They listen. They observe. Body language, eye contact, and behavior tell me so much more than what's written on a piece of paper. It's not foolproof. I've made errors in judgment in the past. But overall, my ability to detect in others the humility and willingness to work has paid off handsomely.

THOSE WITH CHARACTER, APPLY HERE

I've already mentioned one of my heroes, Sir Ernest Shackleton, the British explorer who famously led three expeditions to the Antarctic at the beginning of the last century, had a similar unconventional approach to HR. His recruiting process for the second major expedition of his career—to walk across the South Pole from the Weddell Sea to the Ross Sea—was as much about character as credentials. Some of the crew he hired had never even traveled beyond the British Isles. It was a scientific mission, but when he interviewed physicist Reginald James, one of the few questions he asked him was whether he could sing! (Coincidentally, I always ask my crew if they can sing or play an instrument.) Whatever additional skill sets they needed for the journey, he could teach them. He knew his men would be challenged by extreme hardships, so what mattered more was mettle.

The eyes of the world were on this Imperial Trans-Antarctic Expedition, which began in 1914, right at the beginning of World War I. Back then, in the early part of the last century, global exploration of the farthest reaches of the Earth, whether that was scaling Mount Everest, reaching the North Pole, plunging more than 3,000 feet to the bottom of the ocean off the Bermuda coast, or crossing the South Pacific from Peru on a boat made of bamboo and balsa logs, scientists and adventurers were on a constant quest to learn more about the dimensions, geology, lifeforms, and physical composition of parts of our world to which few, if any, human beings had gone before. So there was a kind of romance to these expeditions, and a feeling that they would somehow advance human knowledge and civilization. It was heady stuff, way beyond the supposed glamour of a reality show about superyachts on the Mediterranean. But, with temperatures typically dipping to minus 70 degrees Fahrenheit and sustained winds of up to 200 miles per hour, this trip wasn't for the average polar bear (or, this being the Antarctic, penguin), so the job candidates had to be bold and risk-taking, but also capable.

"The men selected must be qualified for their work to meet the special polar conditions," Sir Ernest wrote in his account of his first Antarctic expedition. "They must be able to live in harmony for a long period of time, without outside communication. It must be remembered that men whose desires lead them to the untrodden paths of the world have generally marked individuality. Character and temperament are as important as ability. I have to balance my types, their science or seamanship weighs little against the sort of chaps they are."

Specifically, he was looking for people with optimism, patience, imagination, and courage. Based on his previous journey, where he failed to reach his destination, he understood attitude was everything. You can boast all the credentials in the world, but if you allow anxiety, anger, or fear to take over, you can bring down the whole team. So when he interviewed these men, *how* they answered his seemingly random questions was just as important as the content of their answers. He was looking for something. Would the faith he put in them yield a return on investment? To answer that question, he was trying to tap into their spirit.

You can boast all the credentials in the world,
but if you allow anxiety, anger, or fear to take over,
you can bring down the whole team.

MAD, HOPELESS, AND POSSIBLE

There's still some controversy among historians about whether his recruitment ad in the *Times of London*—"Men Wanted for Hazardous Journey"—that I referenced at the beginning of this book even happened. By the time Sir Ernest was preparing for his second trip to the Antarctic he was already a celebrity and, through word of mouth, had already received about 5,000 applications to join him on his ship, *Endurance*, but he only needed 26 crew, plus 26 for the advance ship, the *Aurora*.

He sorted the applications into three piles: "mad, hopeless, and possible." He stayed open to even the most unlikely recruits, although he allegedly turned down three young women who applied, offering to wear britches to fit in with the male crew. I'm not mad at him for that. He was a man of his time, and it was more than 100 years ago. But he was more progressive than his peers with an eye for diamonds in the rough like Frank Wild, who was second-in-command on the excursion—a drifter who went from expedition to expedition and proved himself to be rock steady when it came to running the day-to-day operations of the ship and looking after the welfare of the crew.

Wild, who was put in charge of the men when they were stranded on Elephant Island for 18 months, waiting for a rescue party, never lost faith in Sir Ernest.

"Wild had a rare tact," wrote Thomas Orde-Lees, the crew's storekeeper, "and the happy knack of saying nothing and yet getting people to do things just as he requires them."

Frank Hurley, the expeditions photographer, was another incredible asset who could have easily been dismissed by a more conventional mind. The Australian, who ran away from home at 13, put his life at risk multiple times to get that perfect shot. He ended up becoming the only World War I photographer who took pictures in color. New Zealander Frank Worsley, the captain, was another runaway, apprenticing on a merchant clipper at 16 before joining the Royal Naval Reserve in England. Worsley turned out to be a master navigator and was credited with the success of a later expedition to South Georgia as he deftly sailed 800 miles of the world's most dangerous seas. Even the cook, Charles Green, proved to be a stalwart as he brought together the stressed-out crew for meals three times a day to maintain a sense of normalcy and calm. He even put together a final meal on the *Endurance* as it was being squeezed and broken by the freezing ice floes. If only I had a chef like that in my *Below Deck Mediterranean* galleys!

I could go on. Sir Ernest has inspired many an article and book on leadership. He was the ultimate compassionate yet effective leader who could get others to follow him to the ends of the earth (or General Powell's darkest valley) and trust him enough to camp out for months on a shelf of ice, knowing he wouldn't quit until he found a way to save them. But that extraordinary faith wasn't just a result of his charisma as a captain; it was his sharp sense of the character and potential of the individuals he chose for his expeditions. He was a shrewd judge of his fellow humans. If he were alive today, I can picture him as the CEO of a multinational corporation. He knew exactly what he was looking for and how to get his team to deliver.

What spoke volumes about Sir Ernest's leadership style was the fact that each of the crew members he picked, from the top scientists of the day to the unruly trawler deckhands, went on to lead lives of great accomplishment, serving on multiple expeditions, becoming war heroes or award-winning scholars. He "graduated" them to new levels of greatness.

PERSISTENCE PAYOFF

I can't say I have ever asked my own crew members if they had good teeth or varicose veins, but I like to think I know what to look for beyond the resume, which barely scratches the surface of who someone is. Persistence is one of the qualities that gets my attention and, ultimately, respect.

Sally's qualifications weren't exactly standard, but she had other qualities that caught my attention. In fact, she noticed me first, when I stepped off *Tuscan Sun*, a superyacht that was docked at the marina in Barcelona. This young woman, who had been working as a crew chef on another boat, decided she wanted to further her career in the yachting industry.

The Persian Canadian, who had been managing 250-seat restaurants attached to five-star hotels throughout Canada, had left her career to join her boyfriend Domenic, a maritime engineer who was maintaining *America*—an historic 151-foot schooner that was sitting inside the nearby shipyard. Domenic got Sally a job as a crew chef. Once that contract ended, Sally decided she wanted to take her career in the yachting industry further, and the sight of a female captain intrigued and impressed her. She decided to walk up to me and introduce herself.

When Sally asked me about any openings on my boat for her and her boyfriend, I was kind but noncommittal. I was busy changing seasons and didn't know if there would be any openings at that point. Sally was also green in the industry, and, after a few bad experiences, I had doubts about hiring couples and the dramas that often accompanied a duo working in confined quarters. But my instincts told me to keep an open mind, so I stopped short of saying no.

"Give me your CV and let me think about it," I told her.

Sally kept coming by, hoping I might have an opening for her. After a few more strolls past the dock, it just so happened someone had left my crew and there was a vacancy for a second stew. Sally leaped at the chance, and I took the time to mentor her, allowing her to get her basic safety at sea certification (STCW), along with other certifications that would enable her to multitask on a boat, such as her powerboat license and dive certification. The next season hadn't yet begun, and we were all still in the marina preparing for upcoming charters, so I was happy to give her the time, especially when I observed her great attitude. Determined to vindicate my decision, Sally was all in.

Two weeks into the job, the boat's chef had to leave. Sally stepped in and started cooking for the crew. Having worked alongside some of the best chefs in the business, Sally's culinary skills impressed. She was well-versed in international cuisine, particularly the flavors of the Pacific Rim and the Middle Eastern dishes her mother cooked.

"Sally, I can taste the love that you are putting into this food," I told her. "You have a calling, so you need to go to school; and when you come back, I promise I will hire you as my chef."

Sally went back to Montreal to study at a local culinary institute and proceeded to get one certification after another. She even studied at Thailand's famed Blue Elephant Cooking School before joining a bigger yacht as sous chef. Once Sally reached a level that she felt was worthy of one of my boats, she showed up on the dock again. I hired her as chef on *Pure Bliss,* keeping my promise, and Sally remained in my crew for the next six years.

Leaders need to start casting a wider net as they build their corporate teams and think about how they are going to attract and retain the best. In case you haven't noticed, there is a severe talent shortage in many industries. It's one of the biggest concerns among the CEOs I've met. Businesses can't hire fast enough, and it's holding back growth. But that's just one reason to consider a job candidate who hasn't followed the traditional career path. The different skill sets that people bring when they switch industries can be invaluable as you chart your business course through an age of economic and technological disruption. Of course you may have to invest in more training to bring an outsider up to speed. But it's so worth it. When you've been inside a bubble for too long you risk getting stuck in groupthink or going blind to the bigger picture. Seeking out a fresh perspective enables you to break out of a static mindset and see solutions to problems or more efficient approaches to business that might never have occurred to you. Again, that's the power of diversity in viewpoints, culture, and experience.

To that end, give your potential candidates a second and third look. Obviously if they are totally green and can contribute little of relevance to the enterprise, that's one thing. You need to have at least some decent raw material to mold and shape. But I've never asked for cookie-cutter crew members. I could have easily dismissed Sally as another wannabe yachtie trailing behind her boyfriend. But I try to look beyond the superficial to identify someone's potential and willingness to learn, no matter where they come from. It is the soul I see, not the label or the resume.

RIGHT HAND

With Mark Swanson, my first-ever hire when I was working for John Flynn, it was the way he consistently caught my lines as a dock attendant at the Marriot Marina (now Hilton Ft. Lauderdale Marina), never flustered and always cheerful, that inspired me to take a chance. I paid him $150 to work John's dinner cruises with me, helping me with the lines and all the other deck jobs that needed to be done while I was driving the boat. As we got to know each other I learned he had an interest in engineering, so I encouraged him to go to school. He was obviously bright and capable of so much more than the role of dockhand. He went for it, then came back to me fully qualified to work as an engineer on a superyacht.

Mark joined me full-time as chief engineer on the first *White Star*, a 92-foot Hatteras John had built in 1997. In 2000, when John sold the boat to the late Majid Al Futtaim, the Dubai-based billionaire who became my boss for the next six years, Mark agreed to stay with me. It was good to have a friendly face from home. Mark became my second pair of hands and eyes, like my brother at sea, as the two of us learned and grew together in a more international setting, yachting in the Middle East and Mediterranean for Majid and his clientele. He even shared my passion for motorcycles. We each kept a Ducati on board for some on-land adventures around the South of France and Italy's Amalfi Coast.

Mark was with me as I supervised Majid's second boat built at Trinity Yachts out of New Orleans in 2002. Mark designed the engine room, and I designed the bridge of this second *White Star*, the 157-footer I eventually took on that ill-fated trip through the Red Sea. During the months-long build, I went back to school to upgrade my captain's license and get qualified to drive a boat of that size, and I pushed Mark to do the same. But when the time came to take the boat out of the shipyard and get it to our boss in the Middle East, Mark had met a girl. He wanted to stay stateside and build a "normal" life. I was sad, but I understood, and I was proud of his journey from dockhand to chief engineer on some of the finest superyachts in U.S. waters.

I invested in Mark but, in the end, it was a kind of mutual mentorship. We pushed each other to grow and be better, then we graduated each other.

Mutual Mentorship

Sometimes the investment goes both ways. We teach and inspire each other.

Lizzzie Kritzer, a Manhattan-based entrepreneur and one of my dearest friends, has supported and advised me over the years as I've worked toward building my personal platform and brand. She built her own highly successful promotional products business—Kritzer Marketing—from scratch. An Amazonian beauty with a personality to match, Lizzzie (yes, she really spells her name that way—she's unique) has hustle for days. But she runs her company like I run my boats, giving her employees leeway to make decisions but always being accountable for the final product. She's the captain of her own vessel and has chosen to remain a certain size so that she can give that personal attention to quality control.

Lizzzie always takes my call when I have a practical business question about one of my ventures on land, whether that's the creation of my new animated series for kids, Ocean Rangers, or my I Believe Tour, which seeks to inspire through music and a series of talks by those who've achieved against the odds. And Lizzzie, who is a passionate amateur boater, turns to me for advice on all things nautical. When she wanted to take her boat from Florida up to the Hamptons in New York, she was nervous about making that trip up the Atlantic coast, but I told her to travel in my wake.

"Don't you worry, Lizzzie," I assured her, "I'll be looking over my shoulder to make sure you're okay."

That's what we do for each other. That's what my whole sisterhood of successful women does for each other. We create paths, then stick close by, to make sure we're more than okay.

CHIEF TOILET SCRUBBER

Bianca was another one of my hires who went on to do great things. We first met in 2011, after I'd purchased a yacht with my girlfriend at the time. We called it *Defiance*—a sexy, Italian-made 72-foot speedster we docked in Miami. The plan was to do charters, and we needed a chief stew/first mate, someone willing to assist in every aspect of running the boat. This individual needed to be willing to try everything. Since we'd be spending a lot of time together—days at a time at sea—I also wanted someone compatible.

Bianca sure had the right pedigree. She'd earned a degree in business management from a university in England, where she was from, and had experience working as a flight attendant for Emirates, the Middle East region's leading airline. Operational expertise: check! Top notch service training: check! Global experience: check! Bianca had also been crewing on superyachts since 2008, traveling to all the most exclusive destinations. During the interview, she told me how she started out as a third stew. On *Below Deck Mediterranean*, some of my crew jokingly refer to that position as "laundry bitch." In fact, for Bianca, it meant scrubbing toilets.

"There I was in Monaco, one of the most glamorous places in the world, and I had to clean a lot of loos," she told us in that delightful British accent of hers. "But if I was going be the chief toilet scrubber, they were going to be the cleanest bowls ever!"

Work ethic: check! Positive attitude: check!

Bianca worked her way up to sous chef, then finally chef. She was the whole package. She could do everything! We loved the cut of her jib, so we hired her. But was she fun? Heck, yes! The girl had a bone-dry sense of humor and timing that had me collapsing on the deck in paroxysms of giggles.

SEE IT TO BE IT

It wasn't so much that I had a lot to teach Bianca. She was skilled, resourceful, and experienced. The food she prepared was amazing. One day, hours before a charter, I was scrounging in the galley because I was starving. We couldn't keep excess amounts of food on board because our storage was limited, so she gave me a tiny, cup-sized portion of pasta as I whined.

"Guests first!" she commanded, swatting my hand away from a dish she was in the middle of preparing. Of course she was right.

She had everything it took to make it in any service-oriented industry. But what I *could* teach Bianca was self-confidence. She often commented on how self-assured I seemed as I was docking the boat or dealing with a particularly difficult charter broker. I was constantly under pressure, and people questioned my knowledge and abilities, and she watched to see how it never fazed me. If she could see it in me, there's no reason why she couldn't be *it*, herself.

One day, as we were washing down the deck after a charter, she confided in me that she was feeling unsure about her future. As far as I was concerned, she always had a place on any boat I was captaining, but Bianca was ready to transition to a career on land. Living and working full-time at sea has its limits for most people. It isn't for everyone. Bianca wanted to go ashore to become a charter broker, but she couldn't see herself rising to the top in that highly competitive industry. She was full of negative self-talk, convinced that she'd always be pigeonholed as a pretty face who only knew how to pour a glass of champagne without spilling during a sea swell.

"Bianca, you've got to know that you can do anything," I told her.

I wasn't offering her any deep or original insights—just the truth. Over the years, and for a year alongside me, she'd learned everything there was to know about running a charter. She was detail-oriented, understood service at its highest level, and had a head for the numbers. She could handle a budget and had developed a much deeper understanding of the mechanics of operating a large yacht. Her attitude and creative problem solving were exceptional. She could go far as a broker, but the only thing standing in the way was herself.

"You just have to make the decision, believe, execute, and it will happen," I told her.

It's what I did; it's what has always worked for me, so I meant every word.

"You just have to make the decision, believe,
execute, and it will happen."

Bianca is now a charter broker at Burgess, one of the leading superyacht brokerages in the world, traveling between New York, London, Dubai, and Miami. She connects the wealthiest and most powerful clients with the biggest and most luxurious boats ever built in a multibillion-dollar business, deftly handling the egos of celebrities and CEOs, making them happy while keeping them in line in terms of what is safe, reasonable, and possible.

FEELING THE POWER

I will mentor or encourage anyone who shows a hunger and is willing to do the work. But it goes without saying that I particularly enjoy raising up other women. Malia White, my bosun on the show, was determined to find her place alongside the men as deckhand when she first appeared on the show. Malia had spent her life on the water, participating in the family water sports business, running small charter boats and teaching clients how to scuba dive.

I'd been watching her. Pretty and petite, she carried herself in a way that commanded respect from the occasionally rowdy male crew members on deck that belied her physical appearance. Malia was kind and polite, but she did not take crap from anyone. Above all, she worked her butt off and demonstrated a desire to learn. Being young, she was a little unfocused during that first season. But I had an idea how to change all that. One day, as we were filming in Croatia during Season 2, I called her up to the bridge of the 150-foot *Sirocco*.

"I want you to take this boat off the dock," I told her.

"Captain Sandy, are you serious?"

"Deadly," I answered. "I'll be right by your shoulder, but you can do this."

Until you are at the controls of something that massive, handling engines with thousands in horsepower, captaining a superyacht is more of a concept than a reality. Not only would this give Malia the confidence of knowing she pulled it off, it would also give her a visceral sense of the responsibility. She would be able to literally feel the weight and power of my command beneath her hands. If she could handle millions of dollars' worth of boat, knowing all that can go wrong from a single mistake, and how much it could cost while remaining clear-eyed, calm, and focused, I'd know she was capable. And so would she.

Of course she was nervous, but she executed perfectly. There was a boat right in front of us, but her spatial awareness and reaction times were all I could ask for. She was detail-oriented and paid close attention to my instructions, and she was patient and precise.

Sometimes investing in people is a matter of giving them agency, entrusting them with something they've never done before so that they can build an appreciation of the challenge and develop an understanding of what they need to do to master the skill. Again, leaders, give them something that requires them to stretch. They might not reach the new level right away, but they'll be engaged and incentivized to grow. They may even surprise you.

I've rewarded several of my crew with a turn at the wheel when I've seen their potential and positivity. I even invited a stew with an interest in switching to deck positions to drive the boat. I love empowering my crew. With all that can go wrong, it's understandable that most captains would rather not entrust pulling in and out of the dock to anyone but themselves. I know I am putting myself on the line, although I'm always at the ready to take control if necessary. The return on investment is so worth it. Not only does it attract bright young talent into my industry, it changes lives.

Malia would be the first to tell you that moment was a turning point for her. She suddenly got laser-focused on her career. She wanted to become a captain, and in between seasons went on to get her 200-ton captain's license and certification to become a first officer on any sized boat. She's been captaining boats and getting in her navigation hours all over the world. Once she had that goal, I let her know she could ask me anything.

What you don't see on the show are the hours we spent on the bridge together. I shared stories about my own experiences and gave her plenty of encouragement. We talked about everything from maritime law to the importance of work/life balance, something I continue to struggle with. I'd share insights and provide opportunities to any of my crew who demonstrate the same level of passion and commitment. John Flynn did it for me, and I am doing it for them in multiple ways, whether it's a deck crew member I suspect may be struggling with addiction, or a chief stew I am empowering to lead in her own way, knowing I've got her back.

Malia's been through her own storms, including some roiling waters 60 miles off the coast of Tahiti that resulted in fridges sliding across the galley and crew members and guests vomiting all over the boat. They lost a tender when the force of the waves snapped the line that was tied to the bow, but she remained calm throughout the turbulent seas. In subsequent seasons of the show, Malia held her own with her all-male deckhands, showing an ability to lead that was beyond her years.

"Sandy, I never would have considered this path if it hadn't been for you," she told me.

JUST A TASTE

Not every individual you invest in will show an immediate return. In fact, you may never have the satisfaction of knowing the positive impact you've had. I've put a lot into people financially and emotionally over the years and I'll admit that, at times I've been disappointed. But that's no reason not to continue to try, albeit within certain limits I'll discuss in Chapter 6.

Even if you can imprint a little of yourself onto the soul of another, you're giving and making a difference. It could be something as small as taking two minutes to offer a stranger a few words of advice or encouragement. Even the smallest of gestures can show you care, and that may be all it takes to make someone think twice and stop themselves from going down a more self-destructive path. They will still have to pass through their own storms, but maybe your actions offered them enough shelter to get through to the other side.

A gentleman I met in recovery once told me, "Sandy, you can lead a horse to water, but you can't make them drink. Everyone knows that. But what they don't know is that you can also kick them *into* the water so that they can get a little taste of it, even if it's by accident. Then who knows where or how those droplets will impact them? Meanwhile, you'll have done all you can, and that's enough."

At the time of writing this, I am at the "who knows" stage with Jeremy. He's not speaking to either me or Roberta as he grapples with the loss of his birth mother and a whole host of complex questions. He doesn't know where or what he wants to be. He's an angry young man who is hurting. Maybe he resents the fact that I spent so much time away as he was growing up. Maybe he feels some misplaced guilt about the fact that Roberta got to raise him instead of his mother. Before Jessie passed, they were communicating and making plans together as mother and son. Jeremy was cheated for sure. Whatever the issues are, I know they must be gut-wrenching.

He's now 18 years old with a mind and will of his own, just as I had when I was his age and no one was able to reach me. The difference is that he's got several choices. Whether Jeremy wants to chase his dream of going into the film industry, start a business, or go into the military, I will continue to be there for him. Whatever he wants to do in his life, he can do it. But first he must choose. And, when he finally does decide, I will be there for him every step of the way.

- **Invest in others.** Not only is mentoring important in terms of paying it forward and becoming spiritually whole, as a leader it builds intense loyalty in your crew. By helping others to grow I help to grow myself, my business, and my industry.

- **But make sure they are willing to receive.** Size up your crew by observing closely, noticing their attitude, their enthusiasm for even the smallest of tasks, and the attention they pay to the details.

- **Watch for the tells.** Dive deep into who they are and what motivates them, and watch closely as they answer. Body language, eye contact, and behavior say much more than what's written on a piece of paper.

- **Find the balance between the resume and the person.** Per Sir Ernest, "Character and temperament are as important as ability. I have to balance my types; their science or seamanship weighs little against the sort of chaps they are."

- **Attitude is everything.** You can boast all the credentials in the world, but if you allow anxiety, anger, or fear to take over, you can bring down the whole team. When you ask a question, *how* they answer can be just as important as the content of their answers.

- **Persistence pays.** It shows that the person you are investing in doesn't give up. They have the faith they need to continue to try. Just make the decision, believe, and execute. With commitment, faith, and action, it will surely happen.

- **Give a turn at the wheel.** You can't teach leadership unless you're willing to give up some control. Entrust them with something above their pay grade so that they can develop an understanding of what they need to do to master the skill.

- **Don't expect an immediate or obvious return on investment.** Even if you can imprint just a little of yourself onto the soul of another, you're giving and making a difference. Or kick them into the water for a good soaking and an accidental taste!

- **Grow together.** Sometimes the investment goes both ways. Find mutual mentors to teach and inspire you as well. Graduate each other.

Chapter 5

WORK THAT KNOT!

Every problem has a creative solution.

—DONNA KARAN

Anchors have always been my Achilles heel (well, next to finding decent galley chefs who aren't crazy). They get stuck. They drag. They disappear. To lose one is unthinkable. It is illegal to pull into a harbor without one, and it can cost tens of thousands of euros in fines and replacement costs. A messed-up anchor is not my worst nightmare, but it's right up there.

On one occasion, an anchor picked up a power line off St. Tropez in the French Riviera. Imagine the liability! The deck crew had to jump in the water, tie a line onto the cable, attach it to the other windlass on deck, then haul it up. The idea was to take the weight off the power cable, releasing the anchor so it could be dropped back down, freeing it from the cable. But these maneuvers are risky, because if the chains release in an uncontrolled way they could take off a person's limb. Once free of the tangled mess, my crew lifted anchor again to make sure nothing was attached to it. They spent hours working out the safest way to free it, lifting and releasing without damaging the power cable and leaving thousands of locals without power. Hey, it happens. But, had there been any damage, we would have had to pay for the entire thing.

So many operational glitches can happen in yachting, and each one has tested my captaining skills. Getting through these situations requires plenty of creative problem solving. You can't panic or give up. You need to think clearly and trust that you'll come up with a solution.

So many operational glitches can happen in yachting, and each one has tested my captaining skills. Getting through these situations requires plenty of creative problem solving. You can't panic or give up. You need to think clearly and trust that you'll come up with a solution.

On and offshore, the best leaders prepare for the unthinkable. They have a plan B, C, and D. If you're out with your sales force at a client site meeting, for example, and you sense you are about to lose the deal, you don't panic. You pause, read the room, and pivot in a way that gets the negotiations back on track. As I shared in Chapter 1, you can react in fear or choose courage. The former won't make the sale because people can smell desperation. Be brave and allow your wit, resourcefulness, and humor to rise to the surface and earn the win.

Not that I had a choice with that pesky knot. When an anchor gets stuck or a chain gets tangled, there is so much at stake, from the safety of the souls on board to the possibility of losing an entire charter season. Maintaining a level of calm and optimism while working out the problem in multiple ways is critical to leading through a storm. It takes resolve, energy, and focus to detangle and release an anchor. It also requires an ability to bring your team together, empowering and collaborating with them while working seamlessly through the hours, never allowing frustration to stop them.

A TANGLED MESS

In many ways, the tangled chain of an anchor serves as the perfect metaphor for how to approach a problem from all angles and persist until the chains break free. The point is that, with a never-say-die attitude, no obstacle is insurmountable. It can be frustrating and exhausting to untangle it, but you must lean in to any problem you come up against, reminding everyone why it matters, and encouraging your people to work that knot!

I always share with my crew that it's easy to smile and be in a good mood when everything is going as planned. It's how we show up in moments when it goes south that matters most. It's during the worst of times that you get to choose if you want to character-build and become that person who can maintain calm in the middle of chaos.

Like one evening of a charter when we had to drop both anchors due to the gale-force winds that were predicted. When I went to bed things looked relatively calm. But all through the night, the vessel turned and twisted the anchor chains together so tight it looked impenetrable. This epic chain knot occurred during Season Two of the show, while we were anchored off a remote cove of an island off the coast of Croatia with demanding, hard-partying guests on board and a relatively green crew.

Malia had been on overnight anchor watch, but I didn't blame her for the tangled chain. Boats swing on anchor. It happens. We were a little too close to some craggy rock formations and the winds could have caused the boat to drag, relocate, and get dangerously close. That was my main concern. The Mediterranean can be a treacherous sea with "medicanes" that come out of nowhere. I've been on the Mediterranean when the winds suddenly gusted to 70 and 100 knots, then disappeared almost as soon as they came. It's the weirdest thing, as if the surrounding mountains suddenly burped. But that's not what this was. The churning currents and eddies had been subtly doing damage under the surface, which appeared relatively calm, so it was easy to miss what had been happening. This chain mess just snuck up on us.

It took a total of nine hours working at the chains, much the way you would pull and prod to loosen the tangled strands of a delicate necklace, except that this piece of jewelry weighed 1,100 pounds. Meanwhile, we hired a water taxi to take our patient and inebriated guests, whose stay went seven hours over their original schedule, to the nearest port. We stopped what we were doing and dressed in our whites to give them a proper sendoff, then donned our working uniforms as soon as we waved good-bye.

Next, I invited the internal crew, who could do little to help at this point, to make use of the water toys and enjoy themselves while my deckhands and I took turns laboring under the water or leaning over as far as we could and directing from the starboard side. Yes, it was a mess, but why make everyone else suffer? Panic only makes the situation worse, and I wanted to keep the mood on board as light as possible.

I'd do anything to save an anchor, including cruising to the nearest port by tender to hire deep-sea divers. It is worth investing in a team with the equipment and experience to hoist it up safely from the seabed of some of the deepest waters in Europe. I don't care what it takes. And when any member of my crew questions whether it could be done, I say, "I need assistance, not resistance!" Giving up on that knot is never an option. Instead, you persist, pushing through your exhaustion until you find that opening and it releases, finally surrendering to your will.

QUIET HEROISM

This approach is a huge part of what being a great servant leader is all about. There's a quiet heroism to problem solving for others, whether that's for your boss, your clients, or your crew. Great service doesn't demand accolades; it is its own reward. How satisfying to be able to meet a challenge, solve a riddle, or make those pieces of those puzzles fit, even if you have to jury-rig them together! The satisfaction you get from overcoming a challenge and making a situation better is real, whether you are running a business on land or sea. I apply every bit of my ingenuity, patience, and faith into creating the best experience for everyone, whether that's giving guests the time of their lives or helping the people under me excel and shine, because that is how I would want to be treated or led. And when you succeed, give your team the credit. Leadership is about understanding and demonstrating that teamwork makes the dream work. I always emphasize to my crew that their success is *my* success.

The ancient Chinese philosopher Lao Tzu said, "A leader is best when people barely know [s]he exists, when [her] work is done, [her] aim fulfilled, they will say: we did it ourselves." When the people I am leading and serving feel cared for, respected, and understood, I get the best out of them. With obstacles moved out of their way and problems resolved with minimal fuss, they can perform as their best selves. And our guests are overcome by an expansive, generous mood in that atmosphere of calm and professionalism, which can sure pay off in the tip meeting after a particularly challenging charter! Collectively, we are better, and the rising tide lifts us all!

Without that do-or-die problem-solving mindset, you might as well never leave the dock, because even the easiest journeys aren't without a few hiccups. The sea has a way of bringing aboard the most unexpected challenges. As Francis Stokes, who won a solo race around the world on a 39-foot sailboat, put it: "The sea finds out everything you did wrong." Whatever you didn't tie down properly, whatever engine or hydraulics check wasn't performed, once you're on the water it will fast become a problem.

Navigation is all about shifting and adapting to life's changing circumstances. When you chart your course, you must be prepared to make certain adjustments, because you never know when a storm will form, packing 30 knots or more of wind. There will always be perils at sea, but a good captain can approach the waves, redirecting and guiding her boat into a smoother ride with minimum drama. But staying alert, making good decisions, and leading your crew through to the other side of a storm requires a level of calm and perspective that comes with experience.

That's my sweet spot. If you are in danger, you'd never know it by my deliberately calm demeanor. That doesn't mean I am blasé about threats to safety. But there is something about being in a pressure cooker of a predicament that causes my ADHD brain to hyper focus or as I call it, zero focus. Squirrel Sandy disappears and I come into my own as the leader I was always meant to be. It's as if nothing else exists but the problem to be fixed. Like the time I was sailing near off the Amalfi Coast on the *Tuscan Sun* with charter guests on board and a high-pressure hydraulic hose in the engine room had let go.

Each storm teaches me something new. When the engineer called the bridge to inform me that we had a hydraulic leak, I immediately instructed the crew to don fire gear before they entered the engine room to turn off the valve. As I learned on the Red Sea, hydraulic fluid ignites at a certain temperature. Petroleum-based vapor has a flashpoint, and engine rooms get pretty darn hot. All it takes for that mist to burst into flames is another 130 degrees or so. My next step was to slow my speed, then shift into neutral as the engineer secured the hose. Then my engine crew put on blowers to cool down the equipment. We managed to avoid igniting the engine because we shifted quickly into containment mode. To alleviate the tension, I made it fun, cracking jokes and getting my crew to laugh, because, well, gallows humor. Hey, at least we weren't off the coast of Yemen! Meanwhile, the charter guests were none the wiser. *(What noise? No, everything's fine. Please allow me to top up your glass of Moet!)*

SMOOTHING THE WAY

In my business, problem solving should take place outside the line of vision of owners and charter guests whenever possible. By the time they're aware of a situation, if ever, the solution should be, as the French say, a *fait accompli*. The one word you can never say to a billionaire boat owner is *no*. At that level, they don't want to hear about it. It's all on you to scramble to figure out a way to deliver on their extremely high expectations. When someone is spending that kind of money running and maintaining a superyacht, it doesn't matter what problems come up, or who is at fault, because it's *your* job as captain to solve it. You own that seemingly insurmountable problem, that massive, twisted Gordian knot. But, just like Alexander the Great, you also possess the power to slice through it with bold, decisive action.

In 2000, when I first started working for my uber-wealthy Dubai-based boss, I did plenty of advance research to figure out ways I could get special, priority treatment at dockages throughout the Mediterranean. Money always talked. The most insurmountable obstacle could suddenly disappear from my path when I respond correctly to a dockmaster or a supplier or the maître d' of the top restaurant or the head of a local limo service as I compete with all the other yachts for services and space.

"Sandy, I am a poor man!" said with a sad face and hands cupped together, is code in certain Mediterranean countries for an extremely generous advance tip.

When you're heading into a port to escape a storm, just asking nicely for a slip won't always cut it. I've wined and dined the dock-masters and, yes, handed out envelopes stuffed with greenbacks.

"The owner of the 157-foot yacht I'm captaining may need a slip at the last minute," I'd explain with a big smile on my face. "That's not going to be a problem, is it?"

During Season 4 of *Below Deck Mediterranean*, all the ground-work I'd laid building relationships in ports throughout the Medi-terranean paid off. The wind was against us, and we were running late as we made our way from Monaco to St. Tropez. There was just no way we were going to make it to the harbor before it was due to close at 8 p.m. My showrunner Nadine and the production crew were frantic. They took a tender to one of the coastal towns along the way, then hired a car to try to speed to the dockmaster's office to plead with him to keep it open for us.

By the time they got there, I'd already slipped into the harbor without a problem. All I had to do was call ahead to the harbor-master, whom I'd known for years, have a friendly chat about his wife and kids, then plead for the small favor of staying open for an extra hour. It was one of those occasions asking nicely *did* cut it, because I'd already worked hard to build that relationship. The production crew had no idea I'd already radioed ahead to arrange for the extended hours, and I didn't know they were racing to St. Tropez by land. But I loved the problem-solving initiative they took. It may have been a waste of effort, but the fact that they tried so hard made me proud.

DELICATE DANCE

The smartest CEOs understand the value of external relationships. Over my 20-plus years as a yacht captain in Europe I invested a lot of time and effort in treating the dockworkers and staff well, hosting them at parties on the boat at the end of a charter if we had leftover alcohol, and taking the local agents out to dinner at the best restaurants. I did this wherever we regularly docked. Whatever I could do to generate good will, I did, even at the risk of ruining my waistline with lots of delicious pasta and pizza in Naples. I often broke bread with marina owners who had their fingers on the pulse throughout the Amalfi Coast region. If I wanted anything done that is superyacht related, these were my go-to men. They gave me dockage before anyone else. It's also a delicate dance of helping each other: I bring them business, and, in exchange, they help me solve *my* problems.

One dock owner I've grown particularly fond of is Massimo. He is such a character! He has a team of support staff, all women, who work inside a converted container on the dock. I always felt so sorry for them because, with the hot southern Italian sun beating down on its metal roof all day, the place was sweltering, and the few strategically placed fans did little more than move the heat around like a hair dryer.

"Massimo, your trailer is too hot," I told him. "It's like, 100 degrees. The girls are dying in there!"

One day I offered to buy them a portable air conditioner—the kind with the big hose you stick through the window to extract the hot air.

"Sandy, I will catcha cold," he pleaded. "Please, we donna want the AC!"

"Well that's because you're outside, walking the dock," I told him.

"You Americans and your AC. The fans are good enough."

I guess the lesson there was that there are some problems people don't want you to solve for them! Mind your own side of the street or dock.

I crossed another line with a Mediterranean dock owner I'd built a relationship with when I went to a rival marina, which got mysteriously canceled at the last minute. Then I got a call.

"Ola Sandy! I see your dockage is canceled," he told me.

"How did you know?" I asked, then realized the stupidity of my question as soon it was out of my mouth. Mystery solved.

"All right boss," I told him. "But here's the deal. You guys constantly overcharge us, and I can't keep doing that to my clients. You've got to be fair!"

Silence. I knew the marina owner who shall remain nameless was pissed at me, so I tried to make a deal that would benefit us both.

"I tell you what. Why don't you rebook my dockage, but I'll buy all my fuel from you?"

Later on, I went to his marina to fill up and, as we started to fill our tank, one of his men took the fuel house out of our boat and put it in another boat, then returned the hose to our boat. Lesson learned, to never *not* use this gentleman's services again. It's been a cordial marriage of convenience ever since. And besides, it is much less likely to happen now. The industry has come a long way over the years.

Overall, these carefully nurtured alliances have saved me more than once. Massimo, for example, has been my staunchest ally when it counted most. During the previous charter the engine had been running rough and the turbos blew just as we were getting ready to go into port to drop off our guests. I had to somehow get the disabled boat back from Capri to Naples for repairs within a couple of hours—a tow that could have cost my boss as much 100,000 euros. To save the owner of *Pure Bliss* some money and possibly my job as we were facing a massive financial loss on a million-dollar month-long charter, I made Massimo a proposition:

"Massimo, I know you have two large fishing boats at the dock now. I'll give you a fair price to organize a tow. What you pay them is your business."

"*Si, si, si!*" he said, as excited as if it were Christmas come early (as was I when the insurance company approved the expense).

AGAINST THE CLOCK

Once we got back to Massimo's marina, my engineer Mark and I determined that we would need to change out all the turbos. But this would require dismantling part of the engine—a task that would take some time, and we only had a week to make the repairs.

The predicament we were in was the fault of the turbo manufacturer, but that didn't matter to the vessel's owner, Jim Herbert, whom I mentioned in Chapter 3. We already had one canceled charter and I couldn't afford to lose another. The buck stopped with me, and I knew better than to annoy him with details. I had to act fast. I rallied my crew and engaged them all. I started calling my contacts at the superyacht shipyards in Mississippi and Louisiana to help me locate a guy who could build me a new turbo stat. They found me a guy named Tommy on the "Redneck Riviera" in Texas, who got it done. (At that point I was more willing to trust Texas Tommy than the original turbo manufacturer.) The next challenge was figuring out the best way to get this machinery back into Italy without delay. I was on the phone informing the owner and the broker, and making backup plans just in case we didn't make it.

Once the turbos were ready, I had them shipped to Fort Lauderdale. No way was I going to take the chance of having them get stuck in Italian customs. Instead, I flew back to Florida to personally pick up the new turbos and an American mechanic I knew and trusted to install them. My first stop was TJ Maxx, where I bought two enormous duffel bags to carry the turbos. Then I booked a first-class ticket back to Naples because, back then at least, the airline was less likely to give me a hard time about my bulky carry-on. Creative problem solving at its best.

We made the million-dollar charter. Installing the turbos and making the other engine repairs was a challenge, and we had the clock against us. We were dealing with language barriers, we were exhausted, hungry. And yet the whole time my crew and I were smiling and cracking jokes. We had a rhythm, a goal, and this was crunch time, so we had to work as a team. Once again, in these situations, with that much money at stake, you have a choice: be the calm to help bring focus and clarity to a crisis or be the storm and make the situation worse.

SALVAGE MAFIA

As captain there are stretches when I'm in constant crisis management mode, whether that's suddenly having to replace a temperamental chef during a pandemic, when there is a severe shortage of skilled labor and quarantine rules to follow, or dealing with opportunistic seafarers who claim salvage.

Under maritime law, someone can demand a financial reward for helping another vessel at sea, whether that's recovering a ship after a shipwreck, towing, refloating a vessel, or for doing repairs. There are specialist salvage firms that can claim a reward that may be a percentage of the value of the ship and its contents. In 1989, following a spate of disasters at sea in the 1970s, including some major oil spills from tankers, British Admiralty Court created the International Salvage Convention, which it described it as "a voluntary successful service provided in order to save maritime property in danger at sea, entitling the salvor to a reward." The intention was to incentivize these boats to assist in situations where a coastline might be in danger of contamination, or human lives were at risk. But salvors all over the Mediterranean go by a much looser interpretation, especially when a superyacht crosses their path.

In 2007, when I was captaining the *Tuscan Sun* off the coast of Genoa, someone claimed salvage after I hired them for a simple tow to the port. They essentially held the boat for ransom, demanding 250,000 euros for its release. It wasn't salvage, it was piracy. But they were clever. They knew how wealthy the owners were, how much money was at stake, and how much money an insurance company might be willing to throw at the problem. I found myself in an office onshore, surrounded by a group of gentlemen who were basically mafioso.

"Oh, that's *your* boat?" one of them said to me, sneering at the sight of a female captain. "I hope the owner pays."

Fortunately, the Lloyd's of London maritime insurance company set a price for towing services, and not a penny more. They have a pro forma contract that I have people providing these services to sign. In a way, it takes the matter out of my hands, although it sure doesn't stop these characters from trying!

That's why the insurance company is now my first call when something catastrophic happens, before I even tell the owner what is going on. I learned this important lesson after the fire on the *White Star* in the Red Sea. When I am problem solving, it's good to be creative, but it's also great to know what my parameters are.

There's a little room for negotiation, but it's the insurers who set the prices and the terms, based on the minimum amount they can spend to keep the vessel and souls on board safe. These companies have vast experience, with few disasters at sea they haven't encountered before. They also have top-notch crisis management in house, giving me backup in solving some of my most twisted knots!

Mine isn't the only business where people are problem solving 24-7. Customer-facing industries, like restaurants, where the competitive edge comes from providing excellent service, require the constant attention of servant leaders and problem solvers. During the pandemic, restaurant owners were especially challenged by supply-chain problems, increased costs, constantly shifting safety protocols, capacity constraints, and, above all, staffing shortages. The same has been true of any industry where skilled workers and positive attitudes are precious commodities.

ASKNORMA.COM

Finding talent is an ongoing challenge leaders must face. Hiring the right people and then getting the best out of them can make a business, on land but even more so at sea, where there's nowhere to run. That's why I feel so blessed to have the ultimate problem solver in my life: Norma Trease.

I first met Norma after my experience on the Red Sea, while I was still working on the *White Star*, and we've been the best of friends ever since. She'd heard about what happened to me in the Gulf of Aden and decided to interview me for *Captain's Log* and *Dockwalk*, as well as other magazines that specialize in the yachting business. She put me on the map, lionizing me among my peers, for which I am eternally grateful. But Norma does many other things beyond writing about the maritime industry, and the breadth of experience she brings makes her a lifeline for me and other captains. In fact, during her sailing years, Norma held a captain's license, although she doesn't earn her living at the helm. She knows so much, and has so many contacts, that I jokingly refer to her as AskNorma.com.

A diplomat kid who was born in Paraguay and raised in Paris until her parents moved back to the U.S. as a preteen, Norma first got into boating as a teenager in Annapolis, Maryland, where she befriended someone whose father was a dealer in sailboats. She joined them as they took guests out for overnight trips and taught herself to cook in the galley. It turned out Norma was a natural at entertaining. Her infectious personality also translated into sales, and the budding maritime entrepreneur ended up selling several boats during her senior year of high school.

At 17 she made her first transatlantic crossing and became hooked on the seafaring life. After college she trained to be a chef in Italy, then returned to the states, this time to Fort Lauderdale, where she met the captain of the 80-foot sailing yacht *Lord Jim*, one of the biggest in its day, and spent the next decade traveling around the world as a chef on motor and sail yachts. But Norma was destined for bigger things, and she, like most humans, wanted an actual personal life, so she hung up her galley apron.

"I never liked the idea of my boyfriend also being my captain and my boss," she told me.

Instead, Norma wanted to be her own boss, so she took the $21,000 she'd saved up from tips, salary, and writing gigs to start up a successful crew agency, which she sold, creating a wave of yacht service business sales. She's worked in various consulting roles since, including strategic planning, marketing, management, and even marina development. Norma brokered the sale of *Dockwalk* and founded another magazine—*The Crew Report*—and has contributed to many yachting and financial publications ever since.

Most have one career in a lifetime, two at the most. But I am barely scratching the surface of Norma's diverse experience. If it has anything to do with yachting, Norma's name is all over it. She sits on the board of the prestigious International Superyacht Society and is a fellow member of the International SeaKeepers Society, which raises money for marine science and conservation. Her connections are as vast and deep as the ocean, from the billionaire CEOs who own yachts to investment bankers to environmental scientists to charter brokers and, yes, the best boat crew money can hire.

Norma is the ultimate communicator who speaks five languages, including nautical. All I need to do is make one phone call and she can find me exactly who and what I need within hours or less. I try to spread around the favors I ask of her, but she truly is my secret weapon, whether I am trying to organize a charity event or a second stew for the show. During the global pandemic and the sudden growth spurt of the yachting industry, finding great crew is like mining for gold. Norma only does this one-on-one for a rarefied group of superyacht owners and captains. Thank God I am one of them!

Sometimes you just have to work with what you've got.
People can present as the most complicated
of knots, but you must persist.

I got to know Norma well when she was building a major yacht marina—Marina Port Vell—in Barcelona where I spent a lot of time when I was captaining the *Tuscan Sun*. It was a project full of knots, with many moving parts, but Norma, who had never done commercial project management on a construction site before, somehow got it done. As part of an international team, they were under a lot of scrutiny as they sought approvals to develop part of the original inner harbor of the city, which encompasses Spanish Quay, Fisherman's Quay, and the King's Steps, which are cultural and nautical heritage sites. Norma had to navigate some tricky local politics. The project location was also within sight of Clocktower Quay, an 18th-century clocktower that once marked the entrance to the ancient seaport. Norma had to do a delicate dance between the optimal design of the marina and historical preservation, including ensuring that the design and construction of the new marina buildings would maintain the lines of sight for the clocktower, so that Barcelona citizens and port personnel could continue to enjoy the view.

I truly believe Norma could be the CEO of a major multinational company. She has all the qualities to lead in the corporate world if that were a path she chose for herself. That being said, I sure am glad she's on my speed dial!

ASK, DELEGATE, EMPOWER

Great servant leaders understand they can't do it alone. You need diverse minds, including lateral thinkers, linear thinkers, people with great intuition, analytical brains, or engineers who break things down to build them back up again. The more you can surround yourself with extraordinarily skillful, diplomatic, and insightful people, the better you become at creative problem solving. It takes humility to ask, delegate, and empower others.

And sometimes, you just have to work with what you've got. People can present as the most complicated of knots, but you must persist.

I'm not above helping the stews do the dishes so they can get some rest. I gladly haul boxes of supplies from the dock down to the cockpit and put items neatly away when we have a tight turnaround between charters. I am their leader, but I'm also at their service, much like waiters at the finest restaurants, staying quietly in the background, observing closely and unobtrusively before stepping in at exactly the right time. Some keyboard warriors critiquing the show have called this approach micromanaging. I call it serving through problem solving, and I will never stop.

- **Don't panic; persist.** When faced with a Gordian knot of a problem, you need to think clearly and keep the faith that you'll come up with a solution. It takes resolve, energy, and focus to solve a problem.

- **Work every angle.** With a never-say-die attitude, no obstacle is insurmountable. No matter how frustrated you get, lean in to any problem you come up against, reminding everyone, including yourself, why it matters.

- **Remember to crack a joke or two.** Panic only makes the situation worse. Keep the mood on board as light as possible.

- **"I need assistance, not resistance!"** Don't accept negativity. Giving up on that knot is never an option. Pushing through your exhaustion until you find that opening and it releases, finally surrendering to your will.

- **Great service is its own reward.** How satisfying to be able to meet a challenge or solve a puzzle! The satisfaction you get from overcoming a challenge and making a situation better is real, whether you are running a business on land or sea.

- **Serve those you are leading.** When the people I am leading and serving feel cared for, respected, and empowered, I get the best out of them. With obstacles moved out of their way, they can perform as their best selves so that collectively we can benefit.

- **Prepare to pivot.** When you chart your course, you must prepare to make adjustments, because you never know when a storm will arrive.

- **Get creative.** But know your parameters. There are plenty of unconventional ways to come at a problem, but don't overlook the obvious solutions first. There are few situations most businesses haven't encountered in the past, with guidance and protocols from third parties such as insurance and management companies that exist for good reason.

- **The more diverse minds you have access to, the better.** Great servant leaders understand they can't do it alone. The more you can surround yourself with extraordinarily skillful, resourceful, diplomatic, and insightful people, the more you will evolve as a creative problem solver.

- **Work with what, or who, you've got.** People can present as the most complicated of knots, but you must persist.

- **Don't dictate, hover, or stand in the way.** Be at their service, staying quietly in the background, observing closely and unobtrusively before stepping in at exactly the right time.

Chapter 6

MEET ME ON THE BRIDGE

To command is to serve, nothing more and nothing less.

—ANDRE MALRAUX

About a decade ago, while cruising some VIP charter guests around Italy's Amalfi Coast, I had a gut-wrenching decision to make. My first officer, Ben, who I cared about deeply as a friend, had gotten so drunk while on board that he invited himself to join our passengers at the dinner table and proceeded to behave outrageously. One of the guests mentioned the transgression to me the next morning, and that's when I knew Ben had crossed the line. It was never acceptable to drink on board with charter guests. But Ben had a problem. He was an alcoholic, and I recognized the signs all too well. Ben was great at his job when he was sober. But what if his behavior went beyond telling rude jokes and flirting with the primary's wife? What if he'd done something reckless to endanger the souls on board?

With tears in my eyes, I typed out Ben's resignation letter and called him up to the bridge. When I told him what had happened, he had no recollection. He'd been drinking to the point of blackout. But he accepted my decision without protest. He knew I had no choice but to fire him. His alcoholism made him a liability when safety and service at sea was paramount.

It's my job to help crew members correct course. "Meet me on the bridge" are the last words they want to hear, because it often means they've done something wrong that I *will* address. I do it in the form of constructive criticism, intentionally being firm but fair. In a calm tone I will make clear where they need to improve, then balance the "bollocking" with some encouraging words to remind the crew member that I still have faith. I kick them in the proverbial behind, then I give them a hug, figuratively speaking. (In a professional setting I try to avoid physical contact beyond a handshake; it's overly familiar and risks undermining my position of authority.)

Make no mistake, I will fire or reprimand forcefully when necessary. But the thought of having to be harsh with someone still puts a knot in my stomach. I've done far worse things in my life than some of the things I've chastised my crew for. And I feel passionately about mentoring and helping young deckhands and stews because someone did that for me. When I first started in the industry, I needed someone to believe in me, and John Flynn trusted me not just in terms money or his boat, but with his Ferrari! He knew my thing for fast cars and my history with crashing them, yet he put his baby in my hands, allowing me to drive it into the dealership for servicing.

"You see that one scratch?" he pointed out to me. "That's the only mark on this car, just so we're both clear."

John caught the gearhead glaze in my eyes when I turned the ignition and felt all that 788-horsepower purring at my fingertips, but he allowed me to drive off anyway, and it meant the world to me. Yes, I admit I opened up the engine for a few sneaky minutes on the I-95, and boy did it feel good! But I did it with utmost care. No way was I going to let my boss down.

That's why I invest in others. I give three chances, four if I see real potential. When I was running *Pure Bliss* between 2011 and 2014, I fired and rehired my bosun three times. Freddie, a seasoned deckhand from England, was more than capable and great with guests, but he was a hot mess. Like many yachties, he was also a drinker. I am not suggesting he was ever intoxicated while on duty, but a bad hangover can also impair judgment and performance.

When we were docked in Capri, I felt something massive hit us from the starboard side. I stepped outside the bridge to see what happened and realized it was Freddie who'd just crashed into our yacht with the tender he was trying to dock alongside us. (Superyacht tenders are sizeable boats.) Annoyed, I called him to the bridge to ask him if he needed more lessons on how to dock.

"No, thank you, Captain. I know how to do it. I just wasn't paying attention. My apologies."

"Okay, Freddie, fine. But if there is damage to this boat, I am taking it out of your paycheck."

"Thank you, Captain, it won't happen again."

Later, on a charter in the Caribbean, Freddie ran the tender aground with guests on board. The grazes on the hull were relatively minor, although he managed to damage the propellers. There would have been additional costs if he'd messed up the engine. Meanwhile, we had to rent a tender while ours was being repaired. And God forbid one of the passengers had been hurt as Freddie recklessly drove the boat over the rocks.

Many of Freddie's issues stemmed from lousy self-esteem, to the point, I suspected, of self-sabotage. He was also a hopeless romantic, so what set him off on one of his benders was usually related to a woman he was dating. During one of his firings he looked like such a sad-eyed puppy that I broke my hugging rule, grabbed him, and said, "You may not believe in yourself, but I believe in you!"

That faith got stretched to the breaking point when we were all-hands-on-deck in Palma on the Spanish island of Mallorca, loading the yacht onto the ship for a two-week transatlantic crossing back to Fort Lauderdale. We still had plenty to get done, and there was a time crunch. We didn't have a say on when this ship would set sail. Seven of my crew had been there since 6 a.m., but I was missing the eighth. Where the heck was Freddie? Everyone just shrugged. He was MIA, and no one volunteered where he might be, or why. They liked Freddie because he was adorable, and they didn't want to get him into any more trouble than he already was.

Finally, when the ship was loaded, I spotted Freddie walking toward the dock with his shoulders hunched, looking bedraggled. He knew he was about to get fired.

"Freddie, after you've packed up your clothes, I want you to come and have breakfast with me," I told him. "I want to find out what happened to you, and whether she was worth it."

It turned out she was not. Freddie told me the story of being so intoxicated he couldn't remember how to get back to the boat. He had a massive hangover and was over nine miles from the boat, which was already loaded on the Dockwise transport ship. It was a brutally hot morning, and he'd spent three hours walking and vomiting through the hills and pine forests from her village, getting horribly lost in his still partially drunken state. As the first rays of dawn appeared and lit up the horizon, Freddie thought if he just headed toward the water, he might find his way back to our boat. But as the sun rose higher and the minutes turned into hours, Freddie's heart sank. He knew it was over.

Of course, when I heard the full story, and how hard he tried to get back to us, I felt sorry for him. He was covered in scratches, dirt, and bruises from stumbling through the mountainous brush to get to us.

"I am going to give you one more chance to redeem yourself," I told him. "On the ride back, you must paint the entire engine room, and if I like the job you do by the time we get to the other side, I am going to keep you on."

It was a flawless paint job, so I let him stay. Freddie became one of my most reliable assets. Then he fell in love, for real this time, with a bright young woman, a lawyer-turned-yachtie. They eventually married and moved to Australia. No more crashed tenders that I know of!

TEACHABLE MOMENTS

It's almost always the better course to leverage a situation into a teachable moment that helps the people under my charge grow and get better. This is another aspect of my role as a servant leader. A huge part of my command is helping crew to push themselves ("work that knot!") until a problem is solved. When one of my engineers blew one priming pump after the other, because he forgot to switch them off, I told him, "Okay, that was two. You buy the third." He ended up paying for the third because it ran dry again, but that was the last time it ever happened on his watch.

There was no need to reprimand. Give most people the right tools and incentives and they'll eventually get there. I don't believe in beating people over the head with whatever they've done wrong. Scolding is not my thing. Again, who am I to judge? Once people recognize where they've messed up, which is almost always the second they've been caught, there's little to be gained other than resentment when you rub their noses in their failures or misdeeds.

CHAUFFEUR/COIFFURE?

Whatever the error made by a crew member, I almost always default to a teachable moment. Like the time we were docked at Saint Bart's on New Year's Eve with some very high-profile and high-maintenance clients. From the time we picked them up from the airport in St. Maarten the couple had been bickering. During the whole journey to Saint Bart's, the husband got seasick and was throwing up over the side of the yacht, and the wife seemed permanently annoyed. We were desperate to do something to please them and shift their mood. Scot Fraser, my first mate and a former bartender from Vegas whom you met at the beginning of this book, was relatively new to the yachting industry. He used his best mixology and deejaying skills to get the missus up and dancing and it was starting to work, but it was all-hands-on-deck to put smiles on this miserable couple's faces.

At the last minute our guest informed us that she wanted to get her hair done before everyone headed ashore to enjoy dinner and a fireworks display. We needed to find a hair stylist *stat* to come on board prior to their limousine pickup. This was no easy feat, because hundreds of private yachts were anchored off Saint Bart's at the same time, wanting the same things, every yacht from port to starboard, and the demand for any kind of service was off the charts. My chief stew looked up a local stylist, then I assigned Scot to handle the all-important task of picking him up and taking him back to the boat.

Now Saint Bart's is French-speaking territory, and my crew members' knowledge of the language was nonexistent. But Scot thought he had a pretty good idea what a male stylist in Saint Bart's might look like: fashionably dressed and well-coiffed. The name he'd been given was Jacques, a common-enough French name, so Scot wasn't entirely sure how he was going to identify this guy among the thousands of people milling about on the dock in the countdown to midnight. Scot didn't have a phone on him, much less a phone number. But the stylist had been given a time and location. He'd been told to look for our red shirts with our vessel's name emblazoned on the front and back.

Scot took the tender to the dock to meet him at the rendezvous, where he stood for the next 15 minutes with no hairdresser in sight. The minutes started feeling like hours to Scot, who'd been on eggshells about pleasing these guests the entire charter. Eventually, a man did approach Scot and gave him a look of recognition.

"Are you ready to come on the boat?" Scot asked the gentleman.

"Uh, sure," he told him with a shrug. "But what do you want me to do with my car?"

"Well it's your town," Scot told him. "You know better than I would where to park."

It struck Scot as odd that this gentleman did not have a stylist's bag, and his own hairdo was not exactly on trend. But he gave Scot the right name, he knew the name of our boat, so there was no doubt he was the service provider we had booked. Besides, my first mate had a mission to get him back to the boat as soon as possible, so he set his doubts aside. The "stylist" duly climbed into the tender and Scot sped back to the yacht. The clock was ticking, and he so was anxious to get this task completed that he dismissed any doubts he had flickering in the back of his brain.

As soon as they came on board, I could tell that there had been an extremely unfortunate mix up.

"But I am not the coiffeur, I am the chauffeur!" the gentleman with the potbelly and disheveled combover finally exclaimed.

The look of horror on Scot and my chief stew's faces was priceless. It turned out that my chief stew had confused the word *chauffeur*, for driver, with *coiffeur*, for hair stylist. My chief stew was so mortified, she burst into tears. But the situation was so absurd I couldn't help myself. I burst out laughing.

We teased her and told her she'd have to do our persnickety client's hair, which was a terrifying prospect, although the client ended up doing it herself. When the couple were ready to step out, Scot went back to the dock to return the bewildered driver to land

and take them to the actual chauffeur we had booked. The error added substantially to the agency's billable hours. When we received the invoices, we were on the hook for an extra 3,000 euros! We had to pay for three extra hours of the drivers' time. He was there four hours early because he knew how crazy it gets on New Year's Eve and he wanted to secure a parking spot on the marina. That was on him until our mix-up, then suddenly this man was on the clock.

I did not entirely blame my crew. Things happen when there is a language barrier, on top of the tension and general chaos of the moment. They were so desperate to please these difficult guests. Scot should have listened more closely to his instincts about the guy, but his handheld radio was out of range of our vessel, which was too far around the bay at anchor, so even if he had questions, he couldn't reach us to double check. With the clock ticking and thousands of people roaming the area, he was so focused on getting something done that he had tunnel vision. Scot was a linear thinker, concerned about accomplishing tasks in the right order and on time. But that's a good way to miss important details. In detective school they always tell the trainees to take in their surroundings. When so much is at stake, it pays to observe body language. Open your eyes, ears, and mind while you pause for a moment. Turn up your situational awareness.

When crew members make costly mistakes, I challenge them to fix it. But my Chief Stew was too traumatized by her error and preoccupied with the task of making our guests happy for the remainder of the charter. So Scot gallantly stepped in when I announced:

"I'm not going to pay for this."

I didn't want the client to call his charter broker and accuse me of frivolous spending. It was our mistake, not our charter guests. I don't care how rich they are or whether they could afford it; I take my responsibility for other people's money seriously, as I do their safety.

Scot was apprehensive, but, as he put it to me years later: "Getting that money back could not only win me some points with the Captain, it would also mean more money left over that could possibly go towards the tip!"

In one of Scot's past lives, he'd been a car salesman, so this was his chance to put his negotiating skills to the test.

"Here's what you're going to do, Scot. You're going to call the agent and you're going to negotiate. However long it takes, you are going to talk it down. You're going to fight for it."

After a few hours he reported back to me that he got it down by a few hundred euros. I just smiled and said, "We're not paying a dime over the original estimate."

I advised him to plead with them in total transparency.

They balked at first about a refund but, bless his heart, Scot worked the phone for two more days and got that bill down to 1,000 euros.

Scot stepped up and saved the day. But the overall lesson for my crew was better communication. When we're in international settings where different languages are spoken, and even when we're not, we cannot be afraid to slow down and ask questions. Just say, "Excuse me, I'm sorry, but could you repeat that?" Or you can repeat back what you think you heard and ask for confirmation that you got it right. Do it as many times as it takes to get clarity. And there is no shame in asking someone to speak more slowly. Apologize repeatedly, but don't walk away until you're 100 percent sure. That is how I navigate. If I am not absolutely certain of the channel marker, I stop the vessel so that I don't run aground. Because that certainty is a matter not just of dollars but of safety, of life and death.

Scot went on to earn his 3,000-ton captain's license and has a successful career in the maritime industry managing a fleet of superyachts. He was bright, hardworking, and put every one of these experiences into his memory bank, using them to maximize his potential to the fullest. And my chief stew would never again forget the correct meaning of the words "chauffeur" and "coiffeur"!

As a leader, it doesn't always serve me to pile on. I didn't need to bust on anyone for what had happened. When someone makes a mistake, they usually know it, and an over-the-top reaction from me can be a distraction. It can cause resentment, diverting someone's attention away from their own actions and accountability. It can provide them with an excuse to see themselves as victim instead of addressing the behavior that needs to change.

A few years ago, when I was staying at my friend Dr. Jenn Berman's house in California while she was out of town; her son Max, a high school senior, did not realize I was there. He had a few of his buddies over and he'd turned the living room into a marijuana den.

Now Jenn, who is also in recovery, had strict rules about drugs and alcohol in her home. He knew it; I knew it. All it took was a quick exchange of looks between us for him to send his friends home, put away the weed, and open a few windows to air out the place. I smiled knowingly at him because I knew he already felt bad enough. Nothing more needed to be said.

More than a year later, Jenn found out about the incident, but not from me.

"Why didn't you tell me, Sandy?" she asked.

"I didn't want to be a joy kill," I explained. "Max was safe at home. He has a good compass in his head and he knows right from wrong. What good would it have done to have you flip out anyway? If it's not a thing, don't make it a thing!"

FROM BOW TO STERN

If it's the small stuff, kindly draw their attention to it and give them a chance to correct course. With the possible exception of a spectacularly talented chef, I'd rather have character than skills. Yes, it bothers me when I see toys aren't in the water by the time guests wake up, the beds aren't made while they're at breakfast, or the slide isn't pumped up, but those aren't reasons to go off on someone. Yachts can be learned, stews and deckhands can be trained. I give everyone the information well ahead of time, laying out my expectations, with laminated cheat sheets all over the walls below deck so there's no ambiguity about protocols and procedures. If there are any further questions or they need added support or tools to perform, it's on me to be approachable and provide my team with whatever they need.

There will always be moments where guests give feedback. For the duration of the charter they are, in effect, my boss. As captain I decide anything related to navigation, including whether it's safe to leave the dock, where to anchor, and when to return, because that relates to safety. But I am at their service when it comes to anything related to their comfort and enjoyment—a floating concierge, if you will.

At the end of his cruise along the St. Lucia coast, Jim Herbert, the owner of *Pure Bliss*, the vessel I was captaining, sat me down and gave me some suggestions about where we needed to improve.

He complained that one of the wave runners didn't work. He also pointed out that there was no chocolate on his pillow when his bed was turned down at night. He had a few other comments, and was generally happy, but the overall point was that he expected his trip to exceed the experience he might have at a five-star hotel. Otherwise he might just as well stay ashore.

It was painful to hear, but he was absolutely right. Jim, introduced in Chapter 3, was as much a mentor as a boss, and one of my greatest influences in boating and business along with my first vessel owner, John. I apologized profusely and thanked him for the honest assessment. Business leader to business leader, those were the kind of insights that make me better at what I do. Those issues may have seemed small, but they were important, and real evidence that we weren't providing the level of service he deserved. But I saw this as an opportunity. So, I sat my department heads down, praised them for their hard work, then shared the finance executive's feedback.

"It's me you have to please, because if a client is dissatisfied, I take the full brunt," I told them.

From that point on, Tanya, my chief stew, made walk-throughs of all the cabins to do final inspections every time a cabin was cleaned or given turn-down service. And my first officer made sure the bosun was checking the wave runners, turning them on, and ensuring they always had adequate fuel and oil.

FOLDED TOILET PAPER

Attention to detail mirrors exactly how much you care, in any enterprise. An egg that's not poached to perfection, a stainless-steel rail that's smeared with handprints, a toilet paper roll that has not been neatly folded into a point in a freshly turned down guest cabin . . . these niceties are expected, and they should be. In the yachting world, where charter guests pay for seven-star service, putting care and attention into all those seemingly small things add up to an unforgettable experience on my yacht.

On the other hand, a dish that comes out lukewarm or a delay in getting out all the water toys can also stay in the memory of a guest and reflect poorly on my leadership. It's why I observe closely how my crew operate, from the way the heads (toilets) are cleaned to the way the salt stains are mopped off the deck on the bow. Again, I've done all these tasks myself and will happily step in so that my crew fully understands what my standards are, and why they must always be met.

Attention to detail mirrors exactly how much you care, in any enterprise.

If we are under pressure, you bet your ass I am going to step in and do things the way they are supposed to be done. I will stand there and make sure the food goes out hot. I've worked hard to build my reputation among a clientele that includes billionaires, CEOs, and celebrities, so I won't compromise on excellence of service, safety, or integrity. If things slide and they're not addressed by my crew after the gaps in performance have been made clear, I'll start monitoring closely, keeping track of how many times the same mistake is met. It may be because they are overwhelmed and need help, in which case I'll get it to them. But if their nonperformance is because my instructions are being shrugged off, all bets are off. When I overheard Jim on a phone call say, "Shave five percent of the nonperformers," I realized that as captain I have a fiduciary duty to run the business with the same uncompromising discipline.

That said, if a client is picky, unreasonable, or excessively berating of my crew, I will tactfully take the primary guest aside and let them know that my crew are here to serve, not be verbally abused. As I once said to a client whose guests were bullying the stews, "You're paying $1 million to spend the next month with us, and we want you to have a fabulous time," I told her. "But if you make my crew feel less than, they'll try, but they won't be able to put their heart and soul into all they do for you. It's just the nature of the human spirit."

It was a "meet me at the bridge" moment with a charter guest, which has happened more than once. The client spoke with her guests; they changed their behavior and had the vacation of a lifetime. And my crew never forgot how I had their backs. Or the tip—100,000 euros ($160,000 by the exchange rates at the time). It was the biggest tip we ever had!

I'm also mindful of the fact that many charter guests can be impossible to satisfy. Americans tend to be much more vocal about what they like. If they prefer cream instead of milk in their coffee, and three sugars, not two, they will be sure to let us know in real time. But I prefer it to the approach of some other cultures, where they say nothing, smile stiffly, and complain later. I've worked with some of the best stews in the business, but even they are not mind readers.

That investment I make in others, whether it's through teaching, lending support, or giving them opportunities to redeem themselves, more often than not, yields dividends.

We try to never say no to our guests' requests, even if it means flying in Prince Edward Island Malpeque oysters from across the Atlantic for that night's dinner party, or beluga albino caviar from the Caspian Sea. "No problem!" I tell them. But some of the preference sheets I've seen are insane. How can you possibly win when McFussypants wants gluten-free, vegan, keto, dairy-free pepperoni pizza? Or you're anchored near a remote, unpopulated island in the middle of the Mediterranean, at least two hours' travel time from the nearest port, and a guest suddenly decides she wants to get her hair done and go shopping. Or, true story, a charter guest wanted to make a change to the itinerary, pointing to a place on my navigational chart and saying, "Let's go there!"

"Um, that's 800 miles away," I informed him.

"But it's only an inch on the map!"

I'm the buffer. That kind of stuff is why leaders get paid as well as they do. Bianca, my stew on the yacht I co-owned, is petite, but that didn't stop a guest from plonking huge suitcases in front of her and demanding that she carry them up the passerelle all by herself. At 21 years young, this guest had not yet learned basic human kindness. I watched this scene play out; then, when she walked away, I went up to Bianca and whispered:

"Don't you dare pick those up."

"But Captain, it's my job!" Bianca protested.

"You should have told her you would *help* her take his luggage up," I told her. "You are not the heavy lifting crew."

Bianca kept insisting. She was the client, so she felt obliged to fulfill her request.

"No. That crosses the line, and you deserve to be treated with more respect. Just because you work here doesn't mean it falls on your shoulders. What if you injure yourself? What will happen to the rest of the charter? Never allow yourself to be abused, no matter who it is!"

It was another teachable moment.

That investment I make in others, whether it's through teaching, lending support, or giving them opportunities to redeem themselves, more often than not, yields dividends. When you are scrupulously fair toward the people you lead, they're inspired to exceed your expectations.

Boss or Captain?

While I was researching the subject of leadership for this book, I came across a cool infographic by the global software company Volaris Group.[1] It posed the question: are you a boss or a leader? I won't go through the whole list here, but here are a few contrasting qualities:

A boss is a know-it-all; a leader is always willing to listen.

Bosses talk more than they listen; leaders listen more than they talk.

A boss criticizes; a leader encourages.

Bosses direct; leaders coach.

A boss gives answers; a leader seeks solutions.

Bosses demand results; leaders inspire performance.

It's worth internalizing these subtle but significant differences because it is leaders who breed more leaders. They're about others, not themselves.

---

1   https://explore.volarisgroup.com/volaris-group-blog/difference-between-a-boss-and-a-leader

But whether it's a client or a crew member, I am not going to allow myself to be disrespected, and I am certainly not going to tolerate a situation that can affect safety or impact the quality of service we provide. There are many rules under maritime law, and they exist for a reason. There are so many scenarios that might seem harmless on the face of it but could cascade into some truly hazardous situations. Many times I can't let something slide for liability reasons, and even if I want to give that person another chance, my hands are tied. My top five conditions that require me to call someone to the bridge for a serious talking to include:

1. Reports that a member of my crew is being repeatedly offensive or disruptive to their colleagues

2. Doing something illegal and/or unsafe, like taking drugs onboard, being inebriated while on duty, or willfully neglecting safety procedures

3. Repeated poor performance (usually they'll be told where they're lacking, given some training, and two or three chances to make improvements)

4. A persistent refusal to own it or be held accountable; the words, "It's not my job"

5. Broken trust

Some captains don't have a problem with firing people, but that's never been my thing. For me, being a badass captain is getting to mentor and participate in someone's growth. In all the years I've worked on boats, I've fired no more than 10 people. But, even then, I give chances. And I'm constantly mindful of where the line is between gentle, constructive feedback and letting someone know when I am beyond disappointed.

I will occasionally yell or lose it, but it takes a lot to piss me off to the point of firing someone, because I have been given many chances in my life. Who am I to judge when I've stolen cars, stereos, bikes? I've started bar fights just for the fun of it. I've been arrested 18 times. I could have hurt, maimed, or killed someone besides myself during those DUIs, and I thank God that never happened.

The more troubled someone seems, the more my heart wants to help, within reason. When there is a problem, I want to sit down and have a conversation to get to the bottom of what's troubling my crew members. Then I dig into my past experiences to try to relate, and hopefully share a nugget of insight, because leading with compassion is what I was put here to do. Once we've talked the situation through and I believe we've achieved some sort of alignment on the subject, I go back into captain mode and say, "Okay, here are the next steps." But if I continue to get pushback, if they resist and fail to respect my position as captain, we are done.

SEAWORTHY

So yes, I give chances. But at a certain point they are going to run out. There are legal and safety reasons why keeping a crew member isn't an option. The boat world is much stricter than life onshore. Think about all the rules you have at your place of work, which has an entire HR department making sure there is compliance. Now take that office building and put it in the sea. When you're out there, surrounded by water, it adds a whole new layer of restrictions and duties, because you are in a setting where things could easily escalate to life and death. If God forbid something catastrophic happens to one of the souls on board because of a mistake you or one of your crew has made, it doesn't just ruin your career and it's more than just a slap on the wrist or a fine.

As captain, you are responsible, and you need to prove beyond a reasonable doubt to the insurance company that you are not the one who made the mistake. Beyond the insurance liability, if someone gets hurt or something gets damaged, you could go to jail if you knowingly allow a risky and illegal situation to continue. I've been in court before. You hold your hand up, and you swear in a court of law in front of a federal judge that you're not going to lie.

Scot, my first mate on *The Lady J* whom you first met at the beginning of this book, experienced many firsts during his season crewing for me. I appreciated how hard he was working and how eager he was to learn. He'd worked his way up from deckhand to bosun to first mate, and already earned his 200-ton captain's license. He was constantly studying to upgrade his qualifications and one day take the helm of a superyacht, so I got a kick out of pushing him out of his comfort zone. That opportunity arose again when we hired a new chef while we were docked in Fort Lauderdale. As soon as he boarded the vessel he asked Scot, "Are there any good bars around here?"

Scot knew that couldn't be a good sign. But, you know, chefs. The guy could certainly cook, but he kept going out on the town and returning to the boat blackout drunk. There were three times where he literally stumbled back on deck. On one occasion, his last incident with us, he fell in the marina and nearly drowned. His face all bashed and bloody, he made it back to his cabin and vomited all over his quarters. Not only was he endangering himself with his drunkenness, he was making other crew members uncomfortable. So I made Scot fire him.

"Scot, if you want to be a captain, this is one of the hardest parts of the job, but I know you've got this!"

Scot looked crestfallen. He'd never had to fire anyone in his life. The first time I had to fire someone I almost threw up from the anxiety, so I knew exactly how he felt. But being a captain is not just about taking the helm and feeling the power of the vessel. True leadership is also about shouldering the heaviest, least comfortable responsibilities, like telling someone the unpleasant truth that they've run out of chances and it's time to go. Scot handled the situation like a gentleman, and the drunken chef duly packed up his knives and left the yacht.

Of course, that particular firing needed to happen. He hadn't been with us long and everyone on the vessel wanted him gone. There was no way I was going to risk going to sea with charter guests with someone who was so obviously out of control in their addiction.

There are so many dangers in the yachting world, and I don't just mean the unpredictable seas. People can create some of the worst storms. It's a toxic mix of alcohol, drugs, and people feeling less inhibited in foreign lands that can lead to accidents and tragedies for crew members and charter guests. Local laws and customs can be misunderstood, leading to further complications. There are drownings, rapes, overdoses, and broken limbs from people stumbling up the passerelle after a long night out. One season our producer asked a crew agency in Naples how many times she had to take crew members to hospitals. She told her too many to count.

It's in that context that I must make hard decisions, and I don't have room for errors in judgment. Before I start on a new yacht, I'm required to fill out reams of paperwork for the owner, the management company, and the insurance company that promises I will take good care of that $100 million vessel and its passengers, hiring personnel who are "competent and stable." It's all there in the contract.

I don't think in terms of personality, I think liability. I need backbone and character on board—people who are invested in their job performance. They have to *want* to be there and be willing to pitch in and do the grunt work. I'm pretty good at vetting my own crew and have had few regrets over the years, because most have stayed with me until either the owner sold the vessel or they decided it was time to build a life onshore and settle down.

SHOULDER IT!

I work hard to earn not just respect for the position, but for the person. I also set out to earn the trust of my crew, so that they can believe I will have their backs and give them all the support they need to perform at their highest level. But it goes both ways. When there are excuses, I tell them, "Shoulder it!" It's my way of telling them I know they are strong and capable enough to handle a particular challenge themselves, while at the same time subtly letting them know I don't want to hear any more whining. It's *their* responsibility and they need to get it done. When there's backtalk from crew members who think they know better, I also say, "Leave it on your last boat!"

A producer friend of mine had to learn that lesson when she kept getting pushback from one of her production crew about how to set up the room in the cabin where all the monitors and equipment would go. She'd met this young man while filming in Australia. They'd known each other all of six weeks, for the duration of the shoot, but they greeted each other on this new set in Europe like they were best friends reuniting after years apart—full of hugs and laughter.

It was all rainbows and unicorns until my friend asked this gentleman, who was her subordinate, to do something a certain way, and he answered with, "Yeah, mate, but . . . "

The issue was where a certain bank of equipment was going to be located. She wanted it on one side of the cabin, and he kept insisting it be located on the other side and questioning her reasons. *But she was his boss!* My friend looked disheartened. I could tell she felt like she was being mansplained and disrespected by this kid, but she was so eager to be loved by everyone she tried to be sweet about the situation. This went on for ages until I couldn't take it anymore, and firmly suggested he move the monitor.

He did it without another word. Suddenly, the reason why my producer friend wanted the equipment arranged that way became clear. She had the experience, she knew exactly what she was doing, and she was right. From that moment on, it was obvious she was in charge.

This is why I don't hug in a professional context. It blurs the line and confuses people. They think you're their friend when they are there to do a job, answering to you. I suggested to my friend that she sit everybody down for a team meeting.

"Get the niceties out of the way, then make clear that you are the person calling the shots," I told her. "You can wrap the message in humor. Or try a rhyme:

> I'm number one, and you're number two.
> Do as I say, not what you want to do,
> Because you might be on a superyacht,
> But you'll leave in a canoe!"

Of course you can have fun with members of your team, but when you're the leader there needs to be some separation. Especially when you're a bubbly, cute, and petite woman who looks much younger than her years, like my friend, and you're in charge of a bunch of men from parts of the world where they're not as accustomed to having a female leader and condescension is par for the course. Sorry, mate! You can't be everybody's best friend. Again, the hierarchy is there for a reason.

That said, it can be lonely at the helm. I must be the decider, and the responsibility ultimately rests with me. It's both an honor and a load I must carry. But a vessel's bridge can also be a place of intense beauty, where the Milky Way puts on a spectacular show during those silent hours of anchor watch. And it is in those moments that I recognize the position I am in with immense gratitude, saying to myself, "Wow, I'm really here; I am in command!"

- **Be firm but fair.** Reprimand in the form of constructive criticism. Calmly let them know where they need to improve, then balance the difficult feedback with some encouraging words to let them know you still have faith.

- **Earn trust.** Help them believe you will have their backs and give them all the support they need to perform at their highest level. Show them you know your job to not only instill trust, but inspire them to emulate.

- **Give chances, within reason.** Three chances, four if you see real potential, can yield real dividends, because they'll want to prove you right for investing in them.

- **Leverage teachable moments.** Help the people under your charge to grow and get better by addressing the issue head on, in real time, showing them how you expect the task to be done. Give them the information, cheat sheets, and tools.

- **Choose character over skills.** Skills can be taught. Boats can be learned.

- **Incentivize,** financially or through some other type of award, to encourage them to meet a challenge or solve a problem.

- **Adjust the volume.** There's no need to yell or scold because people almost always know when they've messed up. If it's small stuff, kindly draw their attention to it and give them a chance to correct course. Know where the line is between gentle, constructive feedback and letting someone know when you're beyond disappointed.

- **Think liability, not personality.** As much as you might like your subordinates, don't lose sight of what you are trying to accomplish. If they undermine the mission or compromise safety and assets, it's time to be a leader and say good-bye.

- **Stay on top of the details.** They mirror how much you care. Quietly monitor gaps in performance, tracking to see if they are one-offs (we all make mistakes) or a pattern, then step in to address these slips before they're noticed by clients or customers. But if members of your team shrug off these small things, it's time to take action.

- **Don't accept backtalk or excuses.** Tell them, "Shoulder it!" Let them know *you* know they are strong and capable enough to handle a particular challenge themselves, so no more whining. It's *their* responsibility and they need to get it done. To those who think they know better, "Leave it on your last boat!"

- **Be the buffer.** The buck stops with you, and when a client is dissatisfied, you need to stand up and take the full brunt. A captain is only as good as her crew, so take the shots with the bows.

Chapter 7

PUT ON YOUR WHITES

DIG deep—get deliberate, inspired, and going.

—Brené Brown

Standing out of sight on the aft deck, I watched closely as my first officer received a VIP repeat guest—a patron of the Monaco Grand Prix. This crew member had just been promoted, and he had earned every one of those three bars on his shoulder. He was standing tall, confident, and proud of his accomplishments, waiting for the girls to notice him. Then the client, who was all of five feet tall and bald, with a larger-than-life personality, trotted up the passerelle, clearly excited to start his $500k vacation.

"Hey, mate, will you please clean my shoes?" he asked my first officer in a thick East London accent.

My crew member looked dejected, even a little outraged. A swirl of negative emotions started showing up on his face. Knowing this was not good, I rushed over to the guest, grabbed his shoes, and said, "No problem, sir. We will take care of this right away!" Then I motioned to my first officer to follow me into the lazarette, a storage area aft of the cockpit, and proceeded to clean the shoes myself. I wasn't the least bit upset with the young officer, nor did I ridicule him. Instead, I shared an observation:

"We are in the service business and sometimes what might seem a task beneath you is not the case," I reminded him gently. "Everyone's job here is to provide the client with seven-star service and the best experience possible regardless of what's on your epaulettes."

I wanted this young and promising individual to see that I didn't mind cleaning the guest's shoes. In fact, I was polishing with pride. I wanted him to witness, learn, and grow. This was about demonstrating to the next generation of leaders how to show up through my own actions. He had to understand that, if I see something that needs to be done, I have the humility to get down on my knees and do it, even as captain. Rather than just give them a lick and a promise, I was really freaking cleaning our guest's shoes!

FROM THE HEART

As I shared in Chapter 5, successful leadership is as much about humbling yourself to serve as it is to command. It's also about attitude. That dedication to service must be heartfelt. Whether you are captain or a member of the crew depends upon your willingness to show up and put on your whites, those crisp uniforms that captain and crew wear at the beginning and end of a charter to greet guests and bid them a fond farewell.

In the service business especially, your desire to provide that five-star experience needs to be authentic. Nothing gives me greater pride or satisfaction than seeing a guest's appreciation for something one of my crew has done for them. Even if something isn't executed perfectly, that desire to give someone the best of themselves transmits to others. Positive energy might seem like an abstraction, but it's palpable. It can be felt in the air, and it's more powerful than you know.

The young officer didn't need a major attitude adjustment, only a slight tweak. I just had to remind him of the larger reason why he was there, why we were all there: to serve. When I pitch in to serve wherever and whenever I can, it's an act of selfishness because it brings me joy. I want to bring out their best by setting an example of how I want the world to be. Ultimately, serving to lead, whether you are a third stew or a captain, is not just about actions, but emotions, which will reflect in your eyes, your smile, and every small deed. Showing up and representing must be embraced and felt in your bones.

Of course, you can't always flick it on and off like a switch. Putting on your whites and beaming that smile for guests, setting a table, preparing a great meal, mixing a cocktail, whatever it is, must come from a place of enthusiasm, even love. But let's be real. Some days you need to dig a little deeper to find that desire to serve and connect with others. People can sense it when you're struggling from lack of sleep, a personal problem, health issues, or whatever else is stopping you from being fully present. That's why I insist on plenty of rest for myself and my crew. Working someone beyond their breaking point is something that I learned not to do from my first yacht boss and mentor, John Flynn.

WOMAN OVERBOARD

John and Fran were taking a new boat delivery from North Carolina. It was an opportunity for them to enjoy a trip up along Atlantic coastline, including a few stops in the Florida Keys before doubling back to their home base. That meant 21 days in a row of hard work, constantly answering the demands of my boss with just my first mate, Mark, to help me.

I was relieved when, just as the sun had dipped below the horizon, we finally saw the sea buoy for Fort Lauderdale. I had visions of my head hitting the soft pillow of my comfy bed at home, where I would sleep like the dead, uninterrupted for the next 10 hours. I felt like an ultra-marathon runner limping toward the finish line. Then John yelled up to the bridge:

"Sandy, I want to see the stars!"

Are you kidding me? I thought. *Suddenly you're an astronomer?*

To see any constellations, I'd have to go several miles offshore. The light pollution coming from the city meant we'd have to be halfway to the Bahamas. So I turned to Mark and said, "Take the helm," then marched down to the front of the boat where John was enjoying a glass of champagne.

"John, we are not going out to the stars," I told him.

"Why not?" he asked, clearly annoyed by my defiance.

"I'm tired. I'm done."

"Take the boat out!" he insisted, at full volume this time.

"No, and furthermore, as soon as we are docked, I am walking off this boat and never coming back!"

I meant it. I felt abused. For three weeks it felt like there'd been no consideration for our needs. Mark and I were up at dawn and didn't stop until long after John and Fran had gone to bed. We'd reached a breaking point, but my boss had been so involved in his business activities he didn't notice, and he scolded me as I was walking off the yacht.

"John, I'm not a machine," I explained to him when we finally docked. "And even engines need maintenance. You give them downtime to change their oil and fuel filters."

There was a flicker of recognition across his face that he messed up, but he wasn't quite ready to admit it.

"So take a couple of days off, rent a car, and go to the Keys or something, and in a couple of days we'll talk," he said gruffly. "I'll pay."

"No, John, I don't want your money. You're just not getting it. You pushed me too far this time. I quit!"

Three days later, he called to invite me to lunch. I wouldn't say he begged, exactly, but he made it clear he wanted me to come back.

"You know, John, I love what I do, but we need time off. I get that you have a new boat and you want to use and enjoy it, but there has got to be downtime. When you're sitting at the dock, I need to be able to lay in my bed and have no requests."

Ultimately, I did go back to work for John. He was still a taskmaster, but he finally recognized that I needed to be treated at least as well as his equipment and give me more breaks.

When you're giving all day long, it reaches the point where you've got nothing left. You need to be able to fill the tank back up. That means plenty of rest, self-care, and play time. I don't know whether John was intentional about helping me balance my work routine, but one of the daily tasks he gave me was to swim with his dog, Bailey. His boat was docked in the canal behind his house, and Bailey needed a way of exercising without getting overheated in the hot Florida sun. We tried swimming in the pool together for an hour, but the water wasn't cool and refreshing. It was like a bathtub. So I taught Bailey how to jump in the Intercoastal Waterway by tossing her a Frisbee, and I showed her how to get back up. It was an ingenious way of combining work, exercise, and fun, and one of the favorite parts of my day.

"What are you doing swimming?" Fran asked me one day when she ventured out of their air-conditioned house. "Aren't you supposed to be working?"

She couldn't believe it was part of my job. When I wasn't there, Bailey started jumping into the canal and swimming to their wealthy neighbors' backyards to swim in *their* pools. Fran would get a call from one of them, "Are you missing a dog?" For the longest time she couldn't figure out how Bailey was always escaping.

Boats and people tend to spiral if you don't maintain them. That's why I insist on giving my crew time off, even if it's just 24 hours between charters or 8 hours between shifts. Getting enough sleep at sea is serious business. It's mandatory to have crew members log their hours of rest, in the same way pilots can only work a certain number of hours at a stretch. It's critical for maritime safety to make sure everyone is rested and alert. In fact, the Maritime Labor Convention mandates hours of rest for seafarers.

When people don't sleep, they become reactive. They're on the verge. One wrong word, one request too many, and they could walk. That's where I was with John. I wasn't going to ask anymore. In my head it was over, so I just logged off.

FUEL IN THE TANK

Charters are never easy, nor are they supposed to be. Every task performed on land is 10 times harder at sea. My crew must be constantly "on." That pressure is intensified by the time constraints involved in a charter of a few days for an episode of *Below Deck Mediterranean*, where we only learn the guests preferences the day they arrive. Everyone is expected to perform seven-star service at breakfast, lunch, and dinner; field crazy requests from demanding guests; provide water sports; and host land tours, all the while safely moving the boat between anchors. Somehow, we find time to eat and change uniforms three times a day.

But the weeks-long charters we do in the world of yachting can be especially lonely. My crew have missed weddings, family holidays, and funerals. From the outside looking in, working on a superyacht may look glamorous, but in the real world they desperately miss their friends and family onshore. That's why it's vital that they check in with themselves emotionally, eat right, practice sleep hygiene, exercise, or simply let loose when they can (within reason).

The exotic locations you see on the show look much different from a porthole, and the lights and glamour of Monaco don't seem relevant when you are dealing with the harsh realities of cleaning out the bilge water, scrubbing decks, or dealing with an inconsiderate roommate with whom you share a tiny cabin. You don't get to decide what you eat, what you wear, when you sleep, or when you can come and go. During a charter, there is a hierarchy, and your life is not your own. Small wonder that turnover in my industry is 50 percent!

Floating Springboard

Make no mistake, I am not trying to talk you out of a career in my world. If you have the drive and willingness to craft your own destiny, the maritime industry is the place to do it. There is opportunity for people from all backgrounds, whether that's moving up from third stew to chief stew, or bosun to captain. I am a high-school dropout, but look at me now! People who've graduated from yacht crew positions often go on to build their own businesses in the industry, such as serial entrepreneur and Renaissance woman Norma Trease, or my former right-hand-turned-charter broker Bianca, or Mark, my first first mate, who taught himself to become one of the best boat engineers in the business. People who've crewed for me have gone on to find opportunities in philanthropy, sales, catering, or any business that is driven by stellar service.

Of course, the industry won't give back to you freely. It will eat you up if you don't have what it takes, and you need some luck to meet the right owner or the right crew agency at the right time. You also need to be driven and self-promoting, because no one is going to do that for you. There isn't much of a safety net, like healthcare or employer-matched 401Ks. But if you devote yourself long enough, keeping your distance from the drama, showing up with the right attitude, saving up your tip money, and remembering to practice self-care, yachting will yield a return on all that emotional invest-ment. You'll get back what you put in, and then some, as long as you don't deplete those inner reserves and burn out before your journey at sea is over. Dig deep enough and you'll find that career gold. Just remember to pause every so often and fill that tank!

SOUL PSYCHO

Since getting sober, I've made a point of sticking to healthy habits. I don't always succeed, but I always go back to my internal checklist: *did I get enough sleep, did I exercise, did I make my bed, did I say or do something kind, did I listen to a song or read a passage that inspires me . . . ?* That's why, as I write this, I am 32 years sober. Each new day is a chance to reset and do the big and little things that keep me on this path. But I still get a little wobbly when it comes to my work/life balance. I can get caught up in my enthusiasm for a new project or activity and push myself a little too far.

After my motorbike accident I got serious about my physical health and started going to Soul Cycle—the most addictive form of exercise I've ever tried. It's spin class on steroids. I love everything about it: the pumping music, the collective energy of all the other women and men peddling alongside me, the inspirational instruc-tors. . . . My favorite instructor, Pixie, taught the noon class in Beverly Hills, the five-star epicenter of toned bodies and spin enthu-siasts. About halfway into class I felt odd, light-headed. I couldn't swallow, the center of my chest felt tight, and my heart rate, which I was monitoring on my watch, would not go down.

Of course I realized something was seriously wrong, but I didn't feel like announcing my predicament. The last thing I wanted was to disturb that well-heeled class (thankfully Soul Cycle classes are held in the dark). Instead, I slowed down my peddling, and, as I waited for that last song to play, thought about how I was going to unclip myself without falling over, having recently had ankle surgery. I made it off the bike, discretely slipped outside and onto the street, where I called an Uber (I certainly wasn't going to cause a scene and call 911 in the middle of Wilshire Boulevard). As I was making my way outside the building, I started to feel the tingling in my left arm.

"Take me to the nearest hospital," I told the Uber driver. "I'm having a heart attack!" (Imagine his reaction.)

When they put me on the gurney, I told the nurse, "I don't want to die!" I was worried I was running out of lives when there was so much more for me to do on this earth, and sea.

In fact, what I had was a spontaneous coronary artery dissection (SCAD), which is a tear in the vessels of the heart. It wasn't a blockage because my veins were clean. It was the result of unchecked high blood pressure from the medication I'd been prescribed to help me focus better and the extreme exercise I'd been doing: two things intended to improve my physical and mental fitness, and they almost killed me. They repaired the tear, and I spent four days in the hospital getting my vital signs under control.

It was a loud wake-up call. Both my parents had plenty wrong with them physically, but heart attacks are what ultimately killed them, so these issues run in my family. My other realization was that you don't have to be unhealthy to have a heart attack. But when you ignore the signs, fail to properly check in with yourself, go too hard, whatever it is, you literally empty that tank to the point where you are causing engine damage. I thought I was taking care of myself, but I was obviously failing to fine tune.

SCADs are relatively rare. They happen when two of the three layers that make up the arteries of the heart separate, allowing blood to seep into the space between the layers and build up, preventing regular blood flow, which can cause a heart attack. They tend to happen in younger women who don't have risk factors for heart disease, but they can be deadly all the same.

SELF-CHECK-IN

Today my heart is fine. It took me a few years to come out publicly and share this story with the world because I needed to process what happened. I liked to think of myself as invincible, but I had to admit that it was far from the case. There's a middle ground between hypochondria and paying attention. If something is wrong beyond the usual aches and pains of living you should know your own body and be able to sense it. I needed to learn the subtler signs, know my numbers, and ask for help.

One in five women die every year from heart disease, in part because we don't want to bother anyone. But you can't show up and put on your whites if you don't wake up to live another day! I think God spared me this time so that I could use my platform to remind women to clip off that bike and dial 911 if they feel a pain in their chest. Or, if you're suffering from addiction, depression, or any other mental health issues, you can't lift yourself out of the rut, and every day feels like Groundhog Day, you call the 1-800 number, whatever that may be, you go to a meeting, you call for help!

My doctors banned me from Soul Cycle for 12 weeks following my heart attack. I still love it and go as often as possible. I even bought the bike during the pandemic. But the point is to take in a moderate amount of exercise wherever and whenever I can, not just do extreme bursts whenever. On the yacht there is often exercise equipment, but it could be something as simple as running up and down the stairs from the bridge to the galley, walking a ton when I am onshore, using the exercise ball in my cabin, doing a set of sit-ups or push-ups, or simply jumping into the water or doing a lap around my boat. You don't have to go at it like a weekend warrior maniac, and most of us probably shouldn't. A half an hour every day, no matter how busy you are or exhausted you feel, should be enough for your own engine maintenance.

Music is another form of fuel for me. I keep playlists
of songs to serve different purposes: to inspire,
focus, cheer, or relax me.

I also learned that there are other, healthier ways to manage my ADHD. Nadine, my squirrel sister, and I have each figured out our own tricks to focus without the pills. Nadine's a runner. I'll do a quick jog up the stairs between meetings, or a splash of water on my face to zero in and be present. It helps to know which weaknesses to manage and which strengths to leverage. There are certain strategies for mentally putting on your whites when you have a distracted mind like mine, like ridding your working space of clutter. Stuff in disarray makes my brain spin. That's why you see me mutter under my breath in frustration when one of the *Below Deck Mediterranean* crew leaves the laundry room in chaos or the water toys haven't been neatly put away.

Music is another form of fuel for me. I keep playlists of songs to serve different purposes: to inspire, focus, cheer, or relax me. I'm a Seventies rock girl, and anything by AC/DC (first concert) gets me energized. But I am eclectic in my musical taste. "F**k You" by CeeLo Green gets me through some frustrating moments on the show. Zach Williams's "Chain Breaker" gives me hope. "I Am Here" by Pink wakes me up and reminds me to be present, as does Jeremy Camp's "Keep Me in the Moment." "Driver's Seat" by Sniff 'n' the Tears clears my head. "R.E.S.P.E.C.T." by Aretha Franklin gets me to stand tall. "Hotel California" by the Eagles chills me out, "Take a Letter Maria" by R. B. Greaves makes me smile, and "I Lived" by One Republic, my favorite, is pure inspiration. Sometimes all it takes is putting on my Air Pods for 30 seconds to get me into exactly the right headspace to power through the rest of the day.

When I have more time, I also play. I'm a big kid who loves anything to do with speed or water, preferably both at once. Just a chance to be silly, laugh, dance, or watch someone else's face light up is enough to bring some balance to my life and fill up my tank.

MY TWO JENNIFERS

Dr. Jennifer Berman is one of my playmates. Dr. Jenn is brilliant and charming, and through her urology and women's sexual health practice, has done more for the promotion of women's physical and emotional well-being than anyone I know. You may remember her from an appearance on the show in Season 4, when we were in Cannes. She showed up with gifts of vibrators for everyone, and that scene ended up breaking the Internet!

We are different in so many ways, Jenn and I, but our inner children connect. She brings out the giddy side of me people don't get to see on the show. The subject was serious when we first met on the set of *The Doctors*, which Jenn had been co-hosting. I was one of the guests, there to talk about how my motorbike accident led to a full-body x-ray that revealed a cancerous kidney tumor and saved my life. Prompted by a mutual friend, Jenn knocked on my dressing room door to say hello. It was my first time on live television, so I was nervous, but talking to her instantly put me at ease.

Our upbringings are in no way alike, but we share past childhood trauma and struggles with addiction. We could relate on many levels, although, to be honest, what I enjoy most about Jenn is her ability to bring the frivolity and fun. Our first playdate was a weekend in Fort Lauderdale, soon after we met. We got out on the water, dined at the best seafood restaurants, talked for hours, and laughed nonstop. Jenn has absolutely no filter. She'll say anything to anyone, especially on the topic of sex, which can be both shocking and hilarious. That weekend cemented a lifelong sisterhood.

When I moved to Los Angeles in 2016, Jenn welcomed me and invited me into her own circle of friends. She was the one who introduced me to Soul Cycle (Jenn wasn't with me the day of my SCAD, but she's been by my side putting the word out for women's heart health ever since). Afterward, we'd treat ourselves to ice cream at Häagen Das or a cupcake each at Crumbs Bake Shop, gleefully adding back some of the calories we'd just burned. (That's another thing we share: a sweet tooth.)

So Dr. Jenn is my Soul Cycle sister: full of energy and game for any adventure. But my other Jen, Jennifer Grace, is my *soul* sister. Eloquent and wise, she is one of those friends who grounds me and brings me back to a place of equanimity. We first met in 2014, when I was staying in Newport, Rhode Island, and she was doing a reading of her book, *Directing Your Destiny: How to Become the Writer, Producer, and Director of Your Dreams*. (Funny how certain people come into your life exactly when you need them.) Her book is all about self-leadership and directing your own future, which is a subject close to my heart. After the reading I invited her on my boat, *Defiance*, and it was best friends at first sight.

Jennifer has been there for me through the highs and lows. A few months after we met, I was heartbroken over a messy breakup. I so wanted true love in my life, and this failed romance left me feeling like a wounded animal. I met her in a mall parking lot, got out of car, climbed into hers, and started sobbing. Jennifer listened with empathy, allowing me to be in my feelings. Then she helped me to visualize "my future self"—a woman who was long past the pain of the breakup and thriving in both her career and personal life. While she was doing this, she played me a song, "Gypsy Lady," written by her boyfriend Sevren Sanders, who'd made a demo for Kid Rock. It was an upbeat indie rock song about lovers on a crazy road trip that lifted my mood to the point where I was giggling by the time we pulled out of that parking spot.

Jennifer is the friend who comes into my home with the sage and the angel cards. We meditate together and share our dreams. We are both passionate about helping young people understand that they matter and helping them to develop coping skills to get past anxiety and addiction—tools I've been describing on these pages and that we use ourselves. We talk about the deep stuff: why are we here, what is our purpose in life, how can we use our platform and experience to help and inspire others. She's also the friend who helps me get clear on what truly matters.

In fact, Jennifer was with me when I first came up with the idea for the *I Believe Tour.*

"Now you have this platform, what are you going to do with it?" she challenged me not long after I was cast on the show, when I was experiencing those first wounds of mean tweets and toxic social media commentary. "You're only one of a handful of women who drive these big yachts. You can't have this and not share your wisdom!"

Jennifer, who teaches mindfulness and emotional intelligence courses all over the country, including for the New York Department of Education, was one of my first speakers for the tour. After I spoke about female empowerment and what's possible through self-leadership, she talked about "future-self meditation," which was the subject of her Ted Talk. As she did with me in the parked car, she took the audience on a journey 20 years into their future, to meet their older and wiser, been-there-done-that selves. Jennifer had been practicing this particular meditation for years, but it was years later before we realized the coincidence: on this journey the meditators were supposed to imagine being on a boat with a friendly captain!

PHONE A FRIEND

Randi Gold is my other playmate—that platonic friend on speed dial. She was also there for me when my heart was still healing during the filming of my first season on *Below Deck Mediterranean*, listening with love whenever I needed it. There were moments when I broke down and called her from the bathroom between filming. She picked up no matter what the time difference was.

Randi, who now also has long-term sobriety, happened to be at the same meeting in Fort Lauderdale when she first came into my orbit. Our friendship spans more than a decade. While I started my sober life years earlier and worked my way up, Randi started hers at the height of her career as a television broadcast general manager in a top 10 market. She hit the ground hard, suffering public humiliation when her addiction got her arrested—a moment that made local and national news.

"God did for me what I could not do for myself," she told me, many times.

Like me, she had suffered from past childhood trauma, including seeing her mother die in front of her from a brain aneurysm. Her mom's dying words—"Randi, help me!"—haunted her for years, and she never properly grieved the loss. But, when she stopped numbing herself from the pain and finally got sober, her life truly began. I have always known her extraordinary talent in media and PR. The addiction did not steal that from her. In fact, I consult with her on special events and projects from time to time. We love working and playing together. As Randi's career continues to soar, I could not be more proud of my dearest friend.

Randi knows better than anyone the pain of a harsh spotlight. Early in our relationship, as she struggled with social media attacks from people who did not even know her, I would say, "Don't respond.

You know your truth and the world is *not* your judge and jury." She's given me the same advice many times since.

As my fellow traveler in recovery, Randi knows me on a different level. We've both hit bottom at different points. We both make sobriety our priority. She never minimizes what I am going through, because she's been there. Randi is unfiltered, which I appreciate, most of the time. She has these catch phrases, which I like to call Randi-isms. When she wants to encourage me to speak up, she'll say, "Come on, San, what's on your lung should be on your tongue." I love her blend of serious and silly that lightens the mood while we're hard at work on something. She'll even start rapping with me in the middle of a TV studio with hilarious newly made-up verses to our favorite songs. We laugh, we cry, we play, we help others, and we work!

Randi came into my life at around the same time as my two Jennifers. God gave me this sisterhood for a reason. These are the women in my life who have no agenda. Each one is successful in her own right. They're not interested in knowing me for what I can do for them. We were each other's support system before I became famous, and they are the women I turn to, along with my sister Michelle, when I need to cut through the B.S. and hear the unvarnished truth. They are my smackdown team and a soft place to land. I can be filming on location halfway across the world, at any hour of the day or night, and they take my call. They show up for me, and I show up for them.

HEALTHY SEPARATION

As much as these friendships fill me up, I try to keep them separate and apart from my role as "Captain Sandy." They are my precious inner circle, and our conversations are part of my personal arsenal of coping tools. That's why I choose to protect my private relationships and not entangle them on that occasionally messy fame and career ride.

On the show, you may have noticed that I didn't let my hair down and relax with Dr. Jenn and the guests she brought with her. Just as there is a fourth wall between myself and the production crew when we are filming, there's a subtle layer of formality when I am captain. Boundaries are another aspect of putting on your whites. I groan inwardly when I see members of my crew crossing the line between friendly and engaged to overly familiar. Like the deckhand whose witty banter initially entertained guests until he got too comfortable and invited himself to sit down and have a drink with them. Their frozen smiles and nervous exchange of glances should have been his first clue that it was time to politely withdraw. Showing up for others also means knowing how to read the room.

Bringing people into your life, especially those who exist outside of your industry, can give you a fresh perspective. If they are in different fields, it gives you the opportunity for an inside view of another industry and helps you look at your own profession through a whole new lens.

You keep that healthy separation to protect the integrity of those relationships. It was my job to be rainmaker, for Dr. Jenn and her friends, making recommendations for the best restaurants wherever we docked, but I was never footloose. Of course, Dr. Jenn joined me for a few conversations behind the scenes, but apart from engaging with my guests and enjoying their company when they invited me at mealtimes, I kept it professional, focusing on giving them the best possible time. We can let our hair down later, when we're onshore and in each other's homes, where I'm not Captain Sandy. I'm just Sandy!

Why am I telling you about these friendships? Because we all need people who add something to our lives. There are some so-called friends who drain or diminish you. Being around someone who supports you and makes you laugh and feel good about yourself is like taking a mini vacation. It's a cool dip in the ocean on a searingly hot day. Bringing people into your life, especially those who exist outside of your industry, can give you a fresh perspective. If they are in different fields, it gives you the opportunity for an inside view of another industry and helps you look at your own profession through a whole new lens. Our jobs can swallow us whole, but it doesn't have to be that way. Healthy friendships are one more way to fill the tank.

SERVING AS ONE

Make no mistake, it's not all about you. Yes, putting on your freshly pressed and starched whites starts with the right attitude, which comes from a place of physical and emotional well-being. Self-leadership is foundational to leadership. But in the service business your personal needs do not come first. Showing up for your job, your team, and your customers also entails putting on a uniform. We live in an era where people lead with their identity, whether that's based on race, culture, ability, disability, gender, age, LGBTQ status. But on board, we're all the same.

Our crew comes from all over the world, with many kinds of lived experience. They are all races, creeds, religions, and ideologies. Some don't speak English as their first language, or their version is spoken with an Australian, New Zealand, or South African accent. It doesn't matter. We put on that shirt and we're the *Sirocco*, the *Lady Michelle*, the *White Star*, or whatever vessel it happens to be. We are there at the behest of the owner or the guests we are paid to keep safe, well-fed, hydrated, and entertained.

If it's not a thing, then don't make it a thing! Personally, I've never led with identity. My sexual preference is one small part of who I am: a captain who just happens to be a woman who just happens to love a woman who just happens to be living a life of sobriety and who just happens to be on a reality show. I repeat, on the boats that I captain, whatever tribe you belong to is incidental. We are much more than just one thing, and it's that deliciously diverse mix of talent and experience that makes us so effective at what we do. But at the end of the day we serve as one.

- **Show them how to show up.** Demonstrate to the next generation of leaders how to show up through your own actions. If you see something that needs to be done, lead by example and have the humility to get down on your knees and do it, even as captain. Even if that means cleaning shoes!

- **Serve from the heart.** Whether you are a captain or a member of the crew depends upon your willingness to put on that crisp uniform of willing service. A desire to provide that five-star experience needs to be authentic. Positive energy might seem abstract, but it's more powerful than you know.

- **Maintain your engine.** Some days, that desire to serve and connect with others is harder to find. People can sense when you're struggling from lack of sleep, a personal problem, health issues, or whatever else is stopping you from being fully present. Request that downtime when necessary.

- **Check in with yourself.** Don't empty that tank to the point where you are causing engine damage. Pay attention to the subtle signs, then fine tune, and balance.

- **Squeeze in the self-care.** Don't go crazy to make up for the days of exercise you missed; try to find a balance. A half an hour every day, no matter how busy you are or exhausted you feel, is ideal for your engine maintenance.

- **Banish negativity.** Being around friends who support you, make you laugh, and help you feel good about yourself is another way to fill the tank.

- **Mix it up.** Bringing people into your life, especially if they are in different fields, helps you look at your own profession through a whole new lens.

- **It's not all about you.** Yes, identity matters, but no need to lead with it. On my boat, we all wear the same uniform and serve as one.

Chapter 8

ALL CREW, ALL CREW!

Communication is the real work of leadership.

—Nitin Nohria, Dean of Harvard Business School (2010–2020)

In the middle of the night, we were sailing through the waters of the Windward Passage between the Dominican Republic and Cuba when a boat kept showing up and disappearing on the radar system. It was a small vessel, what's known as a "ghost ship," because it is made of wood and harder to detect, especially at night. It was coming up fast on the stern, and Rob Owen, my first officer on navigation duty, was concerned. Was it a pirate?

He woke me up, and I immediately swung into high alert. Three years earlier, I'd dealt with perilous situations on the Red Sea, so I knew exactly what to do, as did my crew, because I'd trained them for this very thing. We put on all the lights and showed presence on deck and made it look like we had a crew of 20 even though we were just six souls on board. Then each crew member, from the deckhands to stews, grabbed fire hoses, standing at the ready on each side of the boat, from bow to stern, while I called the U.S. Coast Guard.

It looked like the pirates were attempting to cut the tender line and steal it. To deter them, we zigzagged our course, charged our fire hoses with sea water, enabling us to spray at full blast. After a couple of hours, the shady vessel moved away. Our yacht was safely in U.S. waters now, with the Coast Guard boat in view. A crisis was averted because my crew was in perfect sync. They knew exactly what to do without being told, and each one played their part while supporting the other. From the outside looking in, it was as seamless and coordinated as watching a dance, even if the performance was somewhat soggy.

Team building is an art. It doesn't just happen. When individuals get along and work well together, it's a reflection of great leadership. Specifically, it's a result of leading with empathy, figuring out who your teammates are and what motivates them, making them understand and feel understood.

Whether you are running a superyacht or a multinational, leadership is team building, and as such a team builder, I cannot stress enough the importance of establishing trust, respect, and confidence within your team members or crew. Your main responsibility is to the people you lead, choosing what to share with them, how the information will affect them. Will it help you in reaching your destination, or will it cause unrest, fear, and tension? Shielding them from the complaints is one powerful way to earn loyalty, which for me is the most important currency at sea. And people naturally gravitate to the leaders and to the managers who invest in them, giving them ample opportunities to grow and show what they can do.

Of course, that culture of respect, professionalism, and calm rests on your own actions and behaviors as leader. As the boss, owner, or CEO, you have the awesome power and responsibility to influence how things are done. If you want professionalism, you must be professional. If you want accountability, you must model honesty and transparency. If you want a group that's mutually supportive, compassionate, and kind, you must sincerely be all those things and, above all, humble.

STRONGER TOGETHER

After all, a captain is only as good as her team, and a team like the one I had on *Pure Bliss* between 2007 and 2011 was a once-in-a-lifetime experience. Fortunately I also had the support and trust of a great owner, Jim Herbert, who gave me all the resources I needed to hire the best. We went through some extremely challenging times together, but the way we were connected, almost able to read each other's minds and finish each other's sentences, really did feel like bliss. There is something almost spiritual about the way a group of strangers from wildly different backgrounds can come together, have each other's backs, and operate as one, jumping in to help and fill the gaps without having to be asked. The old African proverb, "If you want to go fast, go alone; if you want to go far, go together," is especially relevant to my experiences at sea. A true team, a great crew, can accomplish things as a cohesive unit that are beyond human.

People naturally gravitate to the leaders and to the managers who invest in them, giving them ample opportunities to grow and show what they can do.

How does this happen? Through clear and constant communication, especially early in the team building process. One of the assets I value most in crew members is the ability and willingness to communicate.

I used to take these skills for granted, but I'm noticing fewer and fewer young people have even mastered the basics. They don't even make eye contact to acknowledge something I've said. Maybe it has something to do with the amount of time living and interacting through a digital screen, where facial expression, body language, and tone of voice don't seem to matter unless they're performing for a minute-long TikTok video, which is nothing like real-time conversation. In a post-pandemic world, in-person communication has become even more scarce as we meet up on Zoom or Microsoft Teams.

Have you ever gone up to a service counter, placed an order for something, only to receive a blank expression as the associate takes your credit card then looks back down at her phone? Ideally, she would repeat your order back to you to make it clear she heard what you said, or maybe even write it down, but you'd settle for the barest nod of recognition that you exist. The order invariably comes out with something missing or wrong. That is because she has never been taught the basics of two-way communication. It's not necessarily her fault. She's grown up in a digital world, with her face constantly in her phone. But if she wants to succeed and become a leader herself, she'll have to unlearn some bad habits.

Good Communication Hygiene

Choose your words and make sure you deliver your message in a clear, concise manner.

Make sure you make direct eye contact, so the person can see your mouth moving, they see your eyes, and read your body language.

Have them acknowledge your request.

Read the room before you speak. It's about taking the time and demonstrating exactly what you require from them.

When you establish that type of communication style with your team, they will implement it into their daily lives and beyond work. They may even use these healthy communication habits at home.

A REASSURING VOICE

Good communication was a matter of life and death for me when I was stranded on the Red Sea, desperately trying to get information about what to do about the malfunctioning stabilizers that had caused the engine fire. We didn't know at the time what exactly caused the fire and found out only later after an investigation that it was a defect in metal that was used in the equipment, but that's a story for the next chapter. John Allen, who founded Quantum Marine, the company that produced the stabilizers, was there for me day and night, even though there was a nine-hour time difference between Yemen and Florida. John and his team showed up for me and stayed in constant contact in a way few other companies would.

John realized how isolated and desperate I was, so he stayed with me, even if it was 3 a.m. his time, talking through the problems and trying to find a solution. John's company provided gear for military boats in the neighboring Sultanate of Oman, so he leveraged his contacts there to find a mechanic willing to fly down to us and help me get the water pump working. We developed a closeness, the way people do when they're joined together through surreal and dangerous circumstances. John's voice was the sound of reassurance and home. I looked forward to his calls because, in between information about stabilizers, pumps, bow thrusters, and power packs, he entertained me with stories, cracked jokes, and generally kept me sane. We've been good friends ever since.

I respond well to responsiveness. It shows true respect and a desire to serve. As a leader, I have little patience for those who stall or obstruct with silence. Fans of *Below Deck Mediterranean* often ask me about my pet peeves. There are a few, but one of the biggest is when I call a crew member and they don't answer me. They get so locked into what they are doing that they ignore their radio, leave it somewhere, or turn it off, and that channel of communication gets blocked. If you're with a client, tell me you are with a client, but at least answer the radio, then call me back as soon as you can. What if there's an emergency?

What I need to communicate to you must take priority. I'm sitting on the bridge watching the radar, for example. If there is a massive storm headed our way moving in at 25 knots, we have very little time to secure the vessel before it hits us. That storm could be packing 70-knot-winds or more.

Crew members tend to respond better when they have a more complete understanding of each other's jobs. I also try to give everyone a chance to spend time with me on the bridge, even taking the wheel for a few minutes, conditions permitting. These exchanges are more than just some career-day exercise. They help to eliminate petty rivalries and create a well-oiled machine in terms of the safety and operation of the boat. And the positivity can be felt viscerally by charter guests, who experience seven-star service through the pure joy and passion my crew members feel for their jobs.

This emphasis on communication and mutual understanding equips us to be better at safety and service. I've talked a lot about the threats at sea, and how my crew's quick reactions, courage, and perseverance helped save our vessel and the souls on board. But there are other kinds of storms, and how my crew and I faced them while I was captain of the motor yacht *Pure Bliss* has provided multiple leadership lessons that I often share when I speak in front of CEOs and managers.

I've got stories for days about the time we were berthed in Monaco's Port Hercules, one of the most coveted slips in Monte Carlo because it had the best view of the Nouvelle Chicane, premium real estate on the Circuit de Monaco, where the road goes into serpentine curves at the exit of the tunnel to the port, requiring some serious wrist action as the race drivers negotiate the turns. We hosted a party for the 2011 Formula One race with 150 guests on all three decks, plus a VIP dinner party in one of the cabins. A BBC camera crew was set up on our sundeck to film the races while the fancy people mingled, quaffing Moet & Chandon champagne and eating the hors d'oeuvres we circulated on trays by the crateload (one of the parties was for LVMH, which owns Moet).

THE PRINCE OF MONACO

Our charter client was Tony Hewitt, who made his money in chocolate cakes and became one of the race sponsors. Tony, the fellow who wanted his shoes shined in Chapter 7, was a character—outgoing, friendly, and funny—and extremely popular among the jet set across Europe. Through the yacht event platform he owned, Monaco Kool, he seemed to know everyone, from celebrities to CEOs, and friends of Tony's were always invited during the Grand Prix to watch the preliminaries and finals. During that weekend especially, he was the other prince of Monaco.

But it wasn't like we had weeks to prepare. The yacht Tony had initially booked had fallen through at the last minute. One of our chefs freaked out when he heard what was about to happen and hopped on the next plane home to South America without a word. Another character, this guy compared preparing food with making love. He was hilarious, and a joy to watch.

"I *caress* my pasta," he'd say as he tossed a tray of spaghetti. "Next, I bathe her in perfume," he said as he poured it on—the olive oil, I mean.

Apparently there was a hard cap on how many guests this chef wanted to feed with his caressed and perfumed pasta. The man left us high and dry, which I didn't find especially loving. It's not as if there were many chefs available when there were thousands of other yachts and onshore events demanding first-class catering.

But by then I was rich in contacts through my remaining crew. Hilary, my main chef, and my chief stew, Aoife (pronounced Effie), worked the phones and found someone talented and committed enough to both meet our quality standards and handle the workload. I don't care how talented a chef is, creating sublime food inside a galley is a whole other level that requires strong improvisational skills, work ethic, and ability to work under extreme pressure. My team worked a miracle, and it wouldn't be the first or last time.

I knew what resources we had on board because I communicated with my team. It's not just about learning the vessel, it's about learning the individuals who are in your crew. When I put together a team, I ask myself: *What are their strengths? How can I leverage their different personalities and preferences for the betterment of the whole?* Everyone brings something unique and special, but it's how they all fit together that is when the magic happens. It's on me as captain to bring that curiosity about the people who work under me. I ask questions and listen carefully to the answers. I observe their actions and interactions with myself and each other so that I can know who might thrive in certain situations, and who might be totally overwhelmed and in need of more guidance and help.

To get through that Grand Prix weekend, my crew worked around the clock in shifts. There was no room for error. Any glitch in operations could impact the whole charter. All cabins were full with Tony and his closest friends and family, so there was the regular work of preparing three meals a day, including for our crew, and five-star dinners for Tony's high-level guests. My stews were cleaning cabins, washing sheets and clothing daily, including our uniforms, which need to be cleaned and pressed for three changes a day. For the parties, there were hundreds of cloth napkins and table linens to wash, starch, and press. Imagine if we fell behind on this single task?

Our logistics were at the level of a military-style operation. We weren't right next to a dock, because in Monaco there isn't the land space, yet we had to somehow find the space to store volumes of extra supplies. We had to improvise, using the laundry room for the 300 cases of wine, soda, and water we went through during a 24-hour period, when we had to restock again. We used exterior spaces like the bosun's locker, the anchor locker, and the locker on the back of the lower deck where we kept the water toys, which was cool enough to store items such as fruits and vegetables because no galley fridge could have possibility handled that amount of cold storage.

We planned it all out so the items that needed to be accessed the most frequently were stored in places closest to the action for our crew and the additional catering team we hired to quickly grab whatever was running low above deck. The sun deck was already full of camera equipment, which my engineers had to help set up so that the BBC team could film the race connected to our generators without causing a blackout on the entire vessel.

SOAKING-WET CELEB

Aoife essentially became my chief of operations, choreographing movement throughout *Pure Bliss* so that all the different departments wouldn't collide. In addition to our extra servers, which she had to train in a matter of minutes, there were dozens of security staff on board. They were there to protect the VIPs alongside my deck crew, who had to monitor the perimeter and make sure gatecrashers didn't try to sneak over the railing, which almost did happen. One of my officers, Romiro, was looking over the bow when he saw a man climbing up our Jacob's ladder. Stunned, he wasn't sure how this gentleman planned to get inside once he reached the top because the hole where the chain goes is several more feet from the actual railing. It was a dangerous stunt.

The guy waved at Romiro and asked him to call one of the race drivers on board. It was James Blunt, the singer! He was an invited guest, but he couldn't find a tender to take him to our yacht, so he decided to swim. Romiro helped him safely aboard, and James started circulating in the crowd of partygoers, sopping wet. Nobody batted an eye!

Everyone wanted to be where we were. Monte Carlo and all the yachts jam-packed into the harbor were lit up like giant, glitzy Christmas trees in the middle of May. Music was blaring on loudspeakers while the buzz of conversation, laughter, and clinking glasses filled the flotilla of superyachts in our vicinity. You could almost feel the entire place vibrate with anticipation and excitement.

I watched and stepped in wherever needed, but my crew had this. I marveled at the beautiful flow of the service they provided. Deckhands stepped in as servers when needed. First officers and engineers pitched in and cleared the tables if required. The mission was to support one another and not just stick to a job description.

No one would have guessed at the immense and unrelenting pressure my crew faced for three days straight. Aoife's nickname below deck was Aoife La Loca—"Aoife the crazy one"—because she was constantly running around doing something, yet in front of our guests she was consistently calm and efficient, providing the same level of silver star service she gave to royalty before she became a yachtie.

Aoife had paid her way through college serving and managing in some of the finest restaurants in England. With her business degree, she could have been a top broker in a bank, but she caught the yachtie bug on a trip to Mallorca, where she waltzed into a local yacht club, started chatting with the son of a major movie icon at the bar, and through him met numerous yacht owners around the Balearic Islands of Spain, where she got her first experiences crewing. By the time she came to my vessel in 2011, she was highly seasoned. But she didn't quite believe in herself enough. The professional and highly competent demeanor didn't fully match up with how she felt inside. One charter season with me, that soon changed. Friends, family, and people who have crewed for me joke about how I "Tom Sawyer" people. Remember in Mark Twain's *The Adventures of Tom Sawyer* when Tom had to whitewash a fence? He made it look like so much fun he was able to entice all the neighborhood kids to help him. I guess I just have a way of convincing people that even the hardest task is going to be satisfying. And if they need assistance, I'm there. But more often than not, they don't.

In a way, I was Tom Sawyer-ing Aoife, slyly getting her to perform tasks far out of her comfort zone. I put her in high-pressure situations that would have broken most people, but each time she rose to the challenge. She'd spin below deck like a Tasmanian devil, but it would.all get done at a level of excellence I hadn't seen before. And when she paused enough to look back and see what she'd accomplished against the odds, she could see how her experience on board *Pure Bliss* had added to her problem-solving tool kit. And it was that way with the rest of my *Pure Bliss* department heads. At the end of each long day, we'd meet to delegate everyone's roles and responsibilities for the next 24 hours. I poured my faith in them, clearly communicating my expectations, appreciation, and confidence, and they listened. I used my voice as well as my words, modulating my tone and bringing my authentic feelings of pride and gratitude into every sentence. I wanted them to feel about themselves what I felt.

COMMUNICATION STYLES

There is more than one way to communicate, and it's important to adjust to your audience or circumstance. I don't have to yell to let someone know I am displeased, for example. I can speak calmly, yet with the right vocal inflection I can project a steely, I-mean-business tone that's far more impactful than just getting loud. It's a matter of being present enough to connect with your words, mentally and emotionally.

Aoife also learned how to pivot her communication style by allowing herself to be in the moment. She'd been accustomed to Europeans and Brits who expected that white-glove service that's silent and invisible until they need something, then she'd magically appear and refill a glass of wine or clear a plate. But I taught her that North Americans are far less formal. These charter guests like interaction and tend to be more curious about the lives of the people who are waiting on them, so it's okay to chat briefly about where you're from or share the fact that you also happen to have a dog named Muffin. I only had to explain it once to see Aoife run with it, growing more comfortable as she dexterously handled our wide range of clientele. That young woman, with her posh English accent and refined manners, proved she could banter with the most laid-back Texan. She was the perfect chameleon!

It was because I had crew members like Aoife, Rob, Romiro, and Hilary that I had the confidence to accept the most absurd challenges, whether they involved transporting the vessel or entertaining the most exacting of clients. As their leader, it was my job to inspire my crew to do what I already knew they were capable of doing given the right resources and support. By listening and paying attention, I knew exactly how far I could push these individuals, in the same way I know just how fast and far I can steer a vessel.

I don't know if God was trying to prove a point, but it was when I was captaining *Pure Bliss* that I faced some of my greatest challenges outside of the Red Sea. Without crew like Aoife and my first officer, Rob, I'm not so sure we'd have passed the tests, but He gave me the very people I needed to achieve the seemingly impossible.

THE JIGSAW PUZZLE

We were docked in Fort Lauderdale and getting the vessel ready for transport to Europe for the season when we had a catastrophic pipe burst in our air conditioning system. The whole thing needed to be replaced. Tony Hewitt had booked us again for the Monaco Grand Prix and we did not want to disappoint. I simply *had* to make this charter, which was over 3,500 miles away. With less than one month to get us there and ready to meet Tony's high bar for service, I needed to put a plan in action at once. The shipyard we were docked in informed me it would take them six weeks to complete the repairs, but I only had two weeks before we had to load onto Dockwise, a kind of container ship for large yachts.

I had learned a lot when I oversaw the build of the *White Star* several years prior. One of the lessons I took from that experience was that if you have the supplies and materials, the rest was about the labor. The people! I knew of a shipyard that would allow us to bring in subcontractors, so I called up its managers and asked them to arrange 24 carpenters, 24 plumbers, and 12 electricians. I then phoned the insurance company and notified them to start the processes for a catastrophic mechanical claim that I was about to submit on the owner's behalf. This job was going to cost over $350,000, and I wanted to ensure that Jim, the owner, was protected.

I knew it could be done as long as we had the people to work 24-hour days in three shifts. I also knew what my team was capable of. I put Aoife and my chief engineer, Adrian, in charge of logistics, then told the owner how much money we'd need to invest in manpower and materials to complete the job before our departure date, which could not be changed, because Dockwise had a limited transport schedule. After April there wouldn't be another crossing until September.

Everything was mapped out and ordered with precision. We took every piece of the interior apart, from the wood paneling on the walls to the flooring and carpets, and laid it out on the warehouse floor like pieces of a jigsaw puzzle. We used the opportunity to give everything a professional cleaning and restoration while my engineer pulled out all the piping. About 40 artisans, cleaners, electricians, welders, and plumbers got to work restoring, repairing, and installing the new pipe and AC units, which had to be tested and retested to make sure everything worked. Once everything was reinstalled, we could finish the remaining 10 percent of the job during the crossing. It meant my team wouldn't get the two-week-long vacation they deserved before starting another grueling season, but everyone was so mission-focused they didn't care. On the dawn of our loading date, we were pressure-testing the pipes for leaks and found none. However, in the back of my mind I knew it was too good to be true.

Just because a couple of people say it can't be done doesn't mean it's true. Whether you're running a boat, a chain of restaurants, or a multinational footwear manufacturer, you'll be amazed at what you can accomplish if you have the supplies and materials, put your team in place, give them direction, and do not give up.

We pulled off what every shipyard owner in South Florida told us could never happen. But there was one more hitch. When we did our final inspection, with two hours to go before Dockwise set sail, we noticed that some marble tiles in the guest bathrooms had been chipped. Aoife and I worked the phones, located the original supplier in Miami, then paid someone to drive to our shipyard with five replacement tiles. Our boat was ready for the crossing with just minutes to spare.

Once we arrived at Monaco Grand Prix, I informed Tony of our superhuman effort to get us there and asked him to bear with us.

"Tony, if you see a leak, let us know and we will take care of it immediately," I assured him.

It is my responsibility to inform my client of the possibility of leaks or any other issues, and just as well I did, because of course that's what happened. Yet my crew stayed on top of the glitches, swiftly mobilizing to resolve them before they became visible, and our guests were none the wiser. Every little gusher was dealt with in real time so that our client didn't need to explain to his guest exactly why water was pouring out of the ceiling. We made it through the charter!

The takeaway for my crew was that anything is possible if you remember this:

Just because a couple of people say it can't be done doesn't mean it's true. Whether you're running a boat, a chain of restaurants, or a multinational footwear manufacturer, you'll be amazed at what you can accomplish if you have the supplies and materials, put your team in place, give them direction, and do not give up. Ignore the naysayers, rely on your own resources and skill sets, then do the work.

That jigsaw puzzle in Fort Lauderdale was an example of creative problem solving at its best. But, again, even the most brilliant solution is meaningless unless you can find people with the commitment, perseverance, and communication skills to execute. There's a scene in one of my all-time favorite movies, *Invictus* (not to be confused with the poem), about the first interracial rugby match in South Africa, that perfectly sums up what it is to be the leader of a winning team (the Springboks were also the first South African team in history to win the rugby World Cup). The Nelson Mandela character, played by Morgan Freeman, asks the Matt Damon character, Francois Pienaar, the team captain, about his philosophy on leadership:

"How do you inspire your team to do their best?"

"By example. I've always loved to lead by example."

"So that is right. That is exactly right. But how do you get them to be better than they think they can be?"

"That is very difficult," the captain replies, after a thoughtful pause. "I find inspiration perhaps. How do we inspire ourselves to greatness when nothing less will do? How do we inspire everyone around us? I sometimes think it is by using the work of others."

It's one of many reasons why I never take credit as the leader. And when I introduce myself to charter guests, or any external business contact, I don't say my team works *for* me, I say they work *with* me.

VIEW FROM ABOVE

That's not to say there isn't a certain hierarchy, especially when it comes to communication. You don't get to this level of coordination without a kind of structure, where it's understood what's appropriate to communicate, when, and through what channels. As captain, it's understood that mine is the last word on something. I have the command. In my position, I must rise to have that 30,000-foot-high perspective on what's going on with the charter, the owner, the vessel, the weather—important details that influence my decisions in countless ways. Wherever you happen to be leading, never yield your position. When you've built the trust, respect, and loyalty of your team, you have every right to assert yourself when necessary.

It's my role to do the meta-analysis and direct my crew accordingly, but they don't always have to understand exactly why I am giving them certain commands. I have data spewing at me 24/7. In my cabin, at the foot of my bed, there are control screens: a depth sounder, a wind meter, and a watch keeper to make sure whoever is doing a shift on the bridge stays awake. If they don't hit that thing every 20 minutes, an alarm goes off and wakes me up (which, believe me, is not something they want to happen).

I'm transparent with my crew, but only up to a point, because then it becomes information overload. I give every piece of information relevant to performing a task, with discretion. TMI can be distracting, and I want crew members to be as focused as possible on whatever needs to be done in the present moment. If a client complains, individual team members will only hear about it if I feel it's valid, constructive feedback, because I never want to crush their spirits. And I'll do the worrying about next week's charter or the owner who's eager to cut down on his operating expenses. I will make the big-picture decisions about where to navigate, change course, or even leave the dock based on safety.

I am not just giving orders, I am responsible for everyone in a deep way. I am caring for a group of people in the middle of the ocean, where anything can happen. I need to run the flag inspections, the regulatory inspections, the budget, and all the personnel issues with my crew. I may consult with my first officer, first engineer, chef, or chief stew, but in the end, I will be the one who decides. I'm a huge *Star Trek* fan, and there's a great line spoken by Captain James T. Kirk:

"One of the advantages of being a captain, Doctor, is being able to ask for advice without necessarily having to take it."

That said, leadership is knowing how to bring people along, communicating in a way that inspires them to trust your decision-making, not question it. You cannot execute a vision or complete a mission when you don't have people to follow through. When you express yourself in a way that instills the will to persevere, it's like fuel to those you are leading. It brings out their confidence and collective strengths in a way that's almost superhuman, to the point where they could accomplish anything.

Captain of Care

After a year on Pure Bliss, Aoife got a call from her family. Her father was dying from cancer, and she needed to go home to help look after him in his final months. When I learned she was leaving, I cried, but I understood. Years later, Aoife shared that what she learned from me helped her get through one of the most difficult periods anyone must face in life. As the person responsible for her dad's palliative care at her family's home, she took charge of multiple teams of nurses, aides, social workers, and pain specialists. She comforted her mother and other relatives. She organized this crew around the clock, communicating with them constantly so her father always had someone at his bedside to hold his hand, read to him, or to make sure there were no gaps in his pain meds so that he didn't suffer more than he had to. Aoife was physically and emotionally exhausted as she watched her beloved parent fade away, but she found inner reserves of strength she never knew she had.

"Sandy, if I hadn't had that experience being part of you crew, I don't know how I'd have got through it," she told me. "That year on Pure Bliss gave me the skill set and belief that I could achieve the impossible. You set me up to succeed."

TURKEY DAY

In 2012, on a journey to of all things a boat show in the Caribbean, my *Pure Bliss* crew were relentless in their determination to get us there, despite some of the most roiling seas we've ever experienced together.

The vessel, which was now called the *Lady J*, had just been sold to a new owner, but work needed to be done on the hydraulics. The owner wouldn't hear of it. He wanted it delivered from Florida stat. How we got it there was our problem. As we were nearing the Bahamas, the waves were getting rough, and by 4 a.m. I had that old, familiar feeling.

"Man, something feels wrong!" I told Robert Fisher, my bosun, who was standing next to me on the bridge.

He then went down to the engine room, where he discovered there was a leak in the steering system. With just five days to make our deadline for the charter show, were all out of oil, so we put down anchor at Long Island, Bahamas, about halfway between Nassau and the West Indies. It's a pretty place, full of pristine white sand beaches and not much else. I looked at a paper chart and saw there were two air strips, but they were 40 miles away. I gave $600 to Rob and a deckhand, then instructed them to start walking until they could flag down someone driving a truck. (There wasn't a soul on the beach or anywhere that we could see for miles, much less a vehicle.)

Once they reached the "airport," they had orders to stay there until the plane landed. Not that I had a plane with oil at that point, but I wanted them to be ready because I had a deadline to make. It was Thanksgiving Day and a four-day sail to Antigua, the location of the charter show, which was taking place December 2. If I could get my oil in the next few hours, we might just make it.

With nothing to do but wait, I sent my crew to the beach with a cooler full of beer. By then it was 9 a.m., a little early for alcohol but not after what they went through. After the rough night we'd had, they deserved a break. While they were frolicking on the shore, I called one of my suppliers stateside—a guy named Dave Reeves from Quantum Marine who always answered the phone, even on holidays. Year after year on Thanksgiving I happened to be in need of something, and he was the one person I could count on to not turn me down, even on Turkey Day.

"Hey Dave, it's me! Happy Thanksgiving! Shall we keep our holiday tradition going? I need oil ASAP."

There was some available in the Bahamas, which fortunately doesn't shut down on the U.S. holiday. Dave connected me to his oil guy in Nassau, but he didn't accept credit cards, so I found a plane to charter and asked the pilot for a favor:

"Would you mind putting the oil on your credit card and you'll be paid as soon as you land," I asked him, sweetly.

"No problem!"

Four hours later we had the oil. Robert and the deckhand came back triumphantly in the back of the pickup truck with the drums and some fresh fish, and we greeted them like conquering war heroes. By 9 p.m. we were on our way, well fed from our Thanksgiving fish dinner and back in the storm-tossed seas between Cuba and the Dominican Republic, kitty-corner from Haiti, being chased by pirates—the moment I shared with you at the opening of this chapter. I called the Coast Guard, who informed me that there'd been 90 pirate attempts in the area that month! And who knows how many were successful? We lit up the boat, got out the hoses, and I zig-zagged our course until we lost them, but our trials weren't over yet. Rough seas killed an engine and we had to stop again for repairs. My engineer, who'd been working nonstop, got it fixed in two days—record time! Within the mere 24 hours we had to spare, we reached the Antigua charter show.

We made it. Perseverance, problem solving, and constant communication got us safely from one port to the next. But by the time we finished the season, the boat had suffered plenty of wear and tear. It was long overdue for some serious maintenance and repairs at the Rybovich Shipyard in West Palm Beach.

THE DEVIL'S BACKBONE

Every Caribbean season, the seas are rough! The trade winds are often interrupted from December to February by "Northers," or what are locally known as "Christmas Winds," which blow from the north or northwest. These winds are often accompanied by rain and large waves, also from the north. Our vessel was experiencing yet more hydraulic problems on top of steering problems. The seas were well over 15 feet in Exuma Sound, the route vessels almost always take due to the challenging shallow water across the Devil's Backbone—a shallow section of sea to the north of Eleuthera in the Bahamas. Those waters are spiked with jagged reefs well known for ripping out the bottoms of boats, where parrotfish and stingrays float through coral and sections that are essentially a ship's graveyard. But at that point I had no choice but to risk it.

After staring at the chart marked "mailboat route," which consisted of a narrow channel with shallow depths, I decided to hire a local guide with a prearranged pickup off the coast of Long Island in the Bahamas. It was the right move because had it not been for that guide I would have run aground. You must know your limitations and when to seek help. Local knowledge is the only way to cruise the Backbone.

We made it to Staniel Cay in the Exuma district of the Bahamas (think talcum-powder sands, James Bond, and swimming piglets). But the owner wasn't convinced. Our problems at sea had all stemmed from the fact that the necessary upkeep hadn't been done before we left, and now the hydraulics weren't working. This meant we had no way of lifting both our tenders onto the deck. I usually tow one, but the owner instructed me to tow the two tenders in tandem, despite the risk we would easily lose them in rough seas.

He suggested that I send a crew member out to the tenders every so often to bail. Of course he neither knew nor cared what hazards might be if we encountered 8- or 10-foot seas. If you don't know a profession and you are told something can't be done, don't insist. Ask why it can't be done. Have some humility.

"Not happening," I told him. "I will not risk my crew's lives for a tender."

So we towed the boats. Of course the sea was like a bubbling cauldron the entire journey. We somehow made it without running aground but, oops, we lost a tender! (Six months later it washed up onshore at Long Island, Bahamas.)

Docking safely after some hairy nights at sea, my crew decided to celebrate in the bars of the exclusive resort destination with my blessing. I was only interested in a date with my pillow and was in a deep slumber until a 6 a.m. knock on my door jerked me awake. It was Scot.

"Er, sorry, Captain, but you're not going to like this."

Bleary-eyed, I walked onto the stern of the boat, wading through puddles from the previous night's rain. Our vessel wasn't nearly as waterlogged as our one remaining tender, which was upside down in the water. Two of my crew were in wet suits, like little mermaids trying to turn it upright. When my crew returned from their night out, they noticed that the tide had come up and the boat was sinking, so they untied her.

"Why didn't you wake me up?" I asked Scot. "We could have pumped out the water and saved the engines." (They were outboard motors and still above water at that point.)

"I don't know," he replied, looking sheepish.

I was too exhausted to be angry. Besides, the crew had done their best under near impossible conditions. It was a mistake, a communication breakdown at the end of a long, tough charter season. So I grabbed myself a coffee and watched with resignation as my crew struggled to right the tender with ropes and muscle power. I knew my job as captain of *Lady J* was over.

Eventually I called the owner to let him know what happened.

"I've got good news and bad news," I told him. "The bad news is you lost both tenders. I did warn you that might happen."

"And what's the good news?" he asked.

"You only have to pay a $500 deductible to get new boats."

He was annoyed, of course. But I no longer cared about pleasing him. I was done.

"Well, I guess I should resign as your captain."

"That's probably a good idea," he replied.

I never liked the man's total disregard for the maintenance of the vessel, and I was especially unhappy with his indifference to our safety. What kept me going that whole time was my fondness, respect, and gratitude for my crew. I was saddened by the prospect of breaking us up. These men and women would naturally have to disperse to other boats until I could find my next gig captaining a superyacht. A couple of them might join me on my next boat, but it was how everyone in this particular group fit together, a perfect complement of characters, that made what we had special.

As much as I was able to train, teach, and inspire this diverse bunch of talented, hardworking people from all over the world, they helped me to become the best version of myself as a leader. Our experiences allowed me to see what was possible when crew are willing to listen and grow alongside me. I won't say they were like family, because you can't always tell family members what to do. In many ways, what we had was better. We developed that rare closeness that comes from riding out the storms together, then celebrating when we reached safe harbor. It's a bond that remains to this day.

- **Learn the individuals as well as the vessel.** When a crew gets along and works well together, it's a result of leading with empathy. Communicate clearly and often to figure out who your teammates are and what motivates them. Ask yourself: *What are their strengths? How can I leverage their different personalities and preferences for the betterment of the whole? Do they sing?*

- **Operate as one.** A true team can accomplish so much more than individuals acting on their own. Even a group of strangers can come together, have each other's backs, and operate as one, jumping in to help fill the gaps without having to be asked, accomplishing things that are beyond human.

- **Demand acknowledgment**, under all circumstances. Responsiveness from your crew shows respect and a desire to serve. Even if someone is busy, they owe you an answer as their leader, even if it's just to briefly let you know why they can't talk in that moment. In the hierarchy of communication, you're at the top.

- **Build a matrix of mutual respect**, through job exchanges and other methods of familiarization. Crew members tend to respond better when they have a more complete understanding of each other's jobs.

Once a month I make them switch roles so that they can understand the importance of each position.

- **Inspire and command through voice.** Using vocal power in addition to words shows you mean it. Modulate your tone to bring authentic feelings of pride and gratitude into every sentence when you want to inspire. The same goes for discipline. You don't have to yell to let someone know you mean business. The right vocal inflection can project a steely command.

- **Realize that body language is an actual language.** Be mindful of how you communicate visually and don't allow a situation to become more vocal than necessary.

- **It's not for them to question why.** As leader, it's your role to do the meta-analysis and direct your crew accordingly, but they don't always have to understand exactly why you are giving them certain instructions.

- **Know the line between necessary details and TMI.** Give them all the information they need to perform a task well, but be a buffer against information overload and protect them from negative feedback when it's not constructive.

- **Bring them along.** Communicate in a way that inspires them to trust your decision-making. You cannot execute a vision or complete a mission when you don't have people to follow through. When you express yourself in a way that instills the will to persevere, it's more fuel for those you are leading.

Chapter 9

ROLL WITH IT

The best way out is always through.

—ROBERT FROST

One/one thousand, two/one thousand, three/one thousand . . .

In my head I was counting the full seconds. As I was transporting my boss John Flynn's yacht from Florida to New England, off Cape Canaveral, we got hit by a waterspout. This weather phenomenon, which can happen out of nowhere, is like the funnel of a tornado, except that it's filled with water that the wind has sucked up from the sea, turning it into an actual tower of spinning sea water. Suddenly we went from sunlight to total darkness, and the side of the boat smacked hard into this weather monster. It felt much like crashing into a thick cement wall, except that we had no visibility as we were whipped relentlessly by the wetness and gale force winds.

This might actually be it, I thought to myself.

We rolled back up, only to get slammed back down again. I quickly called my sister Michelle to let her know my longitude and latitude. Next, I called John to give him my last known coordinates. It's what you do when there is a disaster at sea to help the Coast Guard's rescue or recovery mission. It at least gives them a chance of finding the boat and the bodies.

A couple of things can happen when you run into a waterspout at sea. It can pass right over you, doing minimal damage, maybe scattering a few deck chairs and blowing out some port holes. Or it can hit you sideways. That's what happened to us, to the point where the vessel was perpendicular to the surface of the sea. That's when I started counting.

Each boat has a certain roll period depending on its size. That's how long it takes to return to an upright position from a certain angle on the port side and starboard side while rolling. There are a lot of factors at play in terms of roll time, including the size and shape of the hull, the vessel's center of gravity, loading conditions, activity on board, and what type of stabilizers it has, but generally on a larger boat like a typical superyacht 130 to 160 feet in length, that roll time varies from six to eight seconds. Beyond that, you're not coming back up. At that point your boat has capsized and all the souls on board could be lost at sea.

Four/one thousand, five/one thousand, six/one thousand, seven/one thousand . . .

We rolled back up, stayed more or less upright, and I started to breathe again.

My experiences at sea have taught me that setbacks and challenges, whether on water or land, dealing with death, illness, or losses of any kind, are not necessarily within my control. It's not within my power to conquer these raging seas. But I can navigate my vessel in a way that does the least damage. How I come out on the other side is all in the approach.

MEASURE THE WAVE

A waterspout is a relatively rare occurrence, but it has happened to me more than once because it's more common in the waters off the south Atlantic coast, particularly around the Florida Keys. Good captains err on the side of caution when they choose whether to leave the dock. They make a judgment based on the Beaufort Wind Scale, which is a calculation of windspeed according to empirical, observable measures. A measure of less than one on the scale means the sea surface is so calm it looks like a mirror. If it's a four or five, the wind is traveling at anywhere from 11 to 21 knots, or what's described as a moderate to fresh breeze. At this point waves might be one to four feet, with a few white caps—a little choppy but still comfortable. Or four to eight feet, with some spray. Beyond that four or five measure, things can take a serious turn.

But when you're delivering a boat to an owner on a schedule, deciding which number is acceptable can be a tough call. Knowing it's just you and a skeleton crew at most, you might choose to risk a six or seven, covering the boat with aluminum storm covers to protect the windows, which can shatter like glass if a wave hits them hard enough. Even if you leave in a three or four, it can climb to a seven before you reach your destination. And, despite the best navigation equipment on the bridge, Mother Nature can be full of surprises. Storm cells can whip up in no time. A microclimate can brew up waves 25 to 50 feet, with driving sea spray and foam that reduces visibility to almost zero. When those waves hit, it feels like a car crash. It's all I can do to look at my monitors and squint out through the one small port hole, praying to God that the boat will hold together.

Those stormy moments can be both humbling and clarifying. They force you to make some hard choices, crystalizing what's most important in that life-and-death moment. My experiences at sea have taught me that setbacks and challenges, whether on water or land, dealing with death, illness, or losses of any kind, are not necessarily within my control. It's not within my power to conquer these raging seas. But I can navigate my vessel in a way that does the least damage. How I come out on the other side is all in the approach.

MAKING LANDFALL

On land, I've had a belly full of storms. There are hardships in life that can suck up all of your energy, gaslight you, and make you question everything you thought you knew. But they pale in comparison with losing a loved one. I was four years sober, only 29, when my father passed, and it was unexpected. He'd had health issues my whole life, but they were chronic conditions he could have lived with for many more years. But when he was just 54 years old, younger than I am as I write this, he got up at 3:30 one morning to go to work, and while my stepmother Shirley was making him coffee, his heart exploded. He was gone in seconds. The shock of a sudden loss like that is brutal. Only someone who's been through it can understand that special kind of grief.

On the heels of my father's death was the passing of my grandmother, my mom's mom, and one of the few stable and sober members of our family. She was our loving, nurturing rock.

But worse for me was the loss of my mother in 2007. I'd kept my distance from her as I got sober, because Mom didn't exactly mellow with age. Physically, she was falling apart. She had cirrhosis of the liver, the family disease. But, as was the case with my dad, Mom's passing was unexpected. She could have easily lingered a few more years with those conditions, but what killed her was a massive heart attack. There were no bedside tears of remorse. No final words spoken. While we were all scattered in our four corners, attempting to distance ourselves from her dysfunction, Mom, this looming figure in our lives, was suddenly gone, and it haunted me. I was so afraid she wouldn't make it to heaven because of the destructive life she'd led. I just had to know she was with God.

Then, on the second day after her death, she came to me in a dream. Mom was standing on the church steps, looking like the stunning young woman I remembered from my childhood. Everyone who'd passed before her—my uncle Vernon and my grandmother who, though she didn't have a driver's license and had never driven a day in her life, started driving the church bus to come and get me.

"Come home, baby," my mother told me. (In this dream, I was still a little girl.)

"No, I want to ride my bike somewhere," I told her.

I didn't think about that dream again until February 21, 2015. I was riding my motorcycle on the way to a boat show in Miami when a car came out of nowhere and T-boned me. As I was flipping through the air, it occurred to me: *this must be my bike ride.* . . . Everything was slow motion until I landed with a crunch on the asphalt. Lying prostrate on the ground in agony, I believed this was the end. Before I got sober there'd been so many accidents that my friends used to joke that I was a cat with 12 lives. But this crash was so bad that a passing driver who stopped to see what had happened ran away when he caught a glimpse of my bleeding and mangled body on the pavement.

By some miracle I survived. Not only that, a body scan to assess the fractures and breaks in my bones also picked up a mass on one of my kidneys. My medical team was able to remove the cancerous tumor before it metastasized, and I am alive today precisely because of this near-death experience. While I was being transported to the hospital and worked on by EMTs and doctors, drifting in and out of consciousness, I felt peaceful, with a deep knowledge that everything would be okay. It was as if I had somehow traveled outside of my body, and God was giving me further confirmation that my mother was with Him.

CONSCIOUSNESS REGAINED

There were other struggles in my business and personal life that all came to a head when I was coming out of the anesthesia for my cancer surgery. Feeling especially vulnerable, I called on my sisters Sabrina and Kim to help me. They showed up to give me emotional support right when I needed it, and I am eternally grateful. The accident, my brush with mortality (the latest of many), and all the other challenges I faced sharpened my sense of what mattered most and I found a new focus. It may sound counterintuitive, but these setbacks gave me a strange kind of gift. They helped me to rediscover that true north I described back in Chapter 1. Until then, I was all over the place.

In navigational terms, the tool we would use to correct course is the gyrocompass I described at the beginning of this book. At the bridge, we do something called a "compass swing" to find out where our true north lies, then adjust for the variations and deviations caused by all the electronic equipment that surrounds us. When we veer in the wrong direction, we are given what's called a "compass deviation card" upon which we make the correction.

Leaders are human. We all need to recognize that we have certain triggers, things that throw us off, so to keep to our true north we need to give ourselves deviation cards, or little reminders. Triggers can be a lot of things. Maybe it's the way someone approaches you. Maybe a certain tone of voice makes the hairs on the back of your neck stand up because it reminds you of a particularly nasty third-grade teacher. Or maybe you recently had an interaction with a younger person, and you could have sworn he whispered, "Okay, boomer" as you walked away. Mine tend to occur in my personal relationships. Whenever I find myself getting annoyed or something is disrupting my usual calm demeanor, I give myself a deviation card—figuratively speaking—and subtly press pause.

Maybe you're not in a situation where you can look down at your feet. If you're at a conference table, it could be something as simple as a quick scribble on the small notepad they hand out in meetings, squeeze a stress ball, or simply take a breath to break that chain of emotions and reactions. Whatever works. The important thing is to put in those variables, have that moment of recognition, then do whatever you can to get back on course.

My life is a compass. Either I am on my true north path, or I am allowing myself to get turned around by magnetic forces. And sometimes I get handed a big-ass deviation card!

I learned so much in the weeks that followed my motorbike accident. Until then, I was still lacking in self-possession and deferring too much to the opinions and approval of others in my personal business dealings. I was excellent at serving others, but not so much myself. As an entrepreneur, I was putting my own best interests last. My mistake was not giving myself those protections when it came to my own business. Working for myself, I needed those same checks and balances I gave to others. I needed to be my own best client and afford myself the same considerations as I would a charter guest or an owner and invest in myself with that added layer of oversight. I deserved an umbrella.

A case in point: Whenever I am hired as a captain, I insist the owners hire a management company so that they never have to wonder if I am taking their money. The management company also keeps us within the lines of legality so that, whenever I get a dicey request from a charter client, or the owners themselves, like leaving the dock in a seven, I can refer them to that third party's rules and politely explain it's out of my hands.

"Mr. Owner, I can't take that risk with you and your family. The insurance company says no. Sorry!"

This was another hard lesson I needed to learn to become the captain I am today. It starts with looking down at your shoes. Excellence in servant leadership begins with taking a beat and making things right within yourself first.

HIS PLAN

After selling the boat I had no idea what I was going to do next. But just as I learned I was cancer-free and was beginning the process of healing physically, I got a call from Nadine Rajabi, a showrunner at Bravo. Would I consider being a captain for the second season of *Below Deck Mediterranean?*

Nadine, a talented and hilariously funny comedian turned reality-show producer, had gotten my name from a mutual acquaintance: a comic and actress and fellow Floridian whom I'd met at a social event. It was the year Hillary Clinton was running for president and Nadine was intrigued by the "girl power" angle for her show, particularly after hearing about my adventure on the Red Sea.

"Captain Sandy stands for tits," the comedienne told Nadine, using an old urban Miami expression that means "tha s*#t, only better."

"Are you kidding me?," Nadine replied. "Show me this unicorn!"

Nadine did some googling, learning more about my background and the bootstraps way I got into the industry. She learned about the Red Sea, and my employment with Majid in Dubai. As someone whose family was from the Middle East, this fact of my work history blew Nadine's mind. "She's captaining a yacht in a country where they don't even let women drive?" she exclaimed.

Nadine became obsessed with getting me on *Below Deck Mediterranean.* She fought hard to have a female captain represented in a male dominated industry, so when she found me, she fiercely pursued me. The fact that I immediately clicked with Nadine made it hard to say no to her. By June, during the San Diego boat show, I'd made up my mind.

"I can't believe you're going to do that show!" someone exclaimed after hearing my news. "It's going to ruin your career."

"What career?" I shot back.

My big plans to build a business were over. But as far as captaining went, I could step back on a boat the next day. Besides, there was more to this than a spot on a reality show.

"This has landed in my lap for a reason. If God wants me to do this, I'm gonna do it. I'm going to go through the casting process and if I can get it, I'll get it."

I was walking dogs and washing boats when I walked into a marina full of superyachts and John Flynn found me. I wasn't looking for a career captaining superyachts when he sent me to school. Then he sent me out to boat builds, which led to Majid, who elevated my career to a global level. The motorbike accident that nearly killed me helped me find the cancer and saved my life. And the failure of my business forced me to wake up and stop being afraid of putting an end to my power coupledom and standing on my own. It pushed me out because I didn't know how to leave. Then, in short order, came the opportunity to be on a show that would introduce my industry to millions of viewers. I was beginning to think there was a pattern here. Some divine power was clearing the way for me.

The path I follow has always directed me in the sense that, whether it is a left turn or right turn, I take it. I put one foot in front of the other and end up where I am supposed to be, again because I try to follow that inner compass. It was as if every major inflection point in my life, even the most painful losses, were teaching and positioning me for this platform. Loss hit me over the head enough times until I woke up and realized it was His plan, not mine. God was, and is, my navigator, and I am fine with that.

The lawsuit was finalized right before I started filming my first season. By that time I'd fully recovered from my accident and cancer surgery, but being on that set, surrounded by young people and given the opportunity to be both a teacher and leader to my crew healed my heart. There were some bumpy moments in that first season, and many episodes since, but it put my Reach One, Teach One mantra on steroids. Getting to help others grow and see the effect of mentoring grow from a ripple to a killer wave through social media gave me a kick like no other, so I took the great with the bad. (Randi Gold, whom you met in Chapter 7, was my rock during filming.)

Everyone has their own journey, but no matter
how many losses you experience in your life,
you don't have to stay stuck.

THE WORST THAT CAN HAPPEN

Is loss always a good thing? Does it always take you to a better place? I believe so, but not in a way we can always realize as we're fighting through it. You search for the horizon, attempting to push your way forward as the wind whips your face and you get tossed by giant wave after giant wave, but the storm is so intense you can't see it. There are some tragedies that are just too great to see beyond, like the death of a child.

How do you get past something like that? During the pandemic, I heard from so many parents and grandparents who'd lost young people due to suicide and drug overdoses. A close friend lost her teenage son to suicide during the lockdown. That is the worst kind of loss. Imagine the guilt on top of the grief!

Everyone has their own journey, but no matter how many losses you experience in your life, you don't have to stay stuck. Kim and Sabrina are the memory keepers in my family. They hang on to stuff. They have storage units full of papers, pictures, and things from the past. I hang on to nothing. I keep my father's watch and wallet, my mother's baking tins, and maybe a few cards. That's it. The rest I let go. My memory is full of holes partly from addiction, but it's also selective. Sabrina and Kim get frustrated with me because I don't like to dwell on the past. I'm afraid if I do, I'll get sucked back into that dark place I lived in for so long.

FOURTH WALL

I've been blessed with getting sober. I've been given plenty of tools for my toolkit, enabling me to feed my soul and remain unstuck. The first is to seek help. Too many people think they can do it by themselves, but I probably wouldn't be alive today if I hadn't sought help from others. There was a period in my life when I hated myself. I didn't think I deserved love and forgiveness and had to be convinced otherwise by sponsors and members of my recovery community. Why would we have more than one person on this planet if we were able to live by ourselves?

Self-forgiveness is a process. It takes time to recover from a hopeless state of mind and body. I worked the steps one by one. I separated myself from people, places, and things that triggered painful memories. I did the inner work, with countless hours of therapy to heal my soul. Through plenty of couch time I've identified and removed the blocks that kept me from moving forward in my life. I left behind all the hurt and disappointment, which ultimately freed me to meet the love of my life.

GIVE ME GRACE

I believe God has a way of preparing you for "the one." He knew I wasn't ready for her all those years ago. And she wasn't ready for me. We were both being prepared for each other. God waited for us. He gave me opportunities to make different choices and be more conscious, so that when that sweet little Facebook message came across my page, I was open.

Leah, the woman who would later become my life partner, had just caught that first season of *Below Deck Mediterranean* and sent me these simple words:

"Congrats on the show. Many blessings."

That last part caught my eye. I had just been thinking how blessed I was feeling. There was a spiritual element to Leah's note, with no agenda. From one soul to another, asking for nothing for return, she was simply saying she was happy for me. Oh, that's lovely, I thought to myself.

That was in June of 2018. It wasn't until October of that year that I checked my Facebook messages. Leah had sent me a link to her music, and her voice gave me chills. She was also gorgeous. I decided to invite her to perform on my *I Believe Tour*, where I use music along with life experiences of those who have overcome to inspire and empower others. That same month, I flew Leah to Los Angeles to meet with her in person. It was love at first sight. We hugged, and we've been together ever since. By 2019 we were living together at her home in Denver.

My relationship with Leah has taught me grace. Until she came into my life, I never fully understood the true meaning of the word. When someone is having a bad day, you don't chide them or try to make them stop whatever it is they are doing that's manifesting the bad mood. Instead, you give them grace and let them have that bad day without judgment. If I am doing something that's not nice, I ask Leah, "Can I have a do over?" That's something I taught her. She gives me that do over, but she gives it with grace. She doesn't constantly remind me, she doesn't add it to a list of grievances, and she doesn't hold me to court.

Leah is God's gift to me. I've always been deeply spiritual, but there is something about her faith that makes me feel more settled, more grounded. She makes me feel like I have found my way home.

BIGGER THAN ME

There is nothing about this journey I would change because it has brought me to where I am today. Finally, I surrendered to a power that's greater than myself. Call it whatever you like: God, nature, the collective good. . . . It was, and is, a matter of somehow aligning my consciousness with something that exists on a higher plane, whatever that is, and continuing to work with others to keep me accountable to myself. This fit spiritual condition takes self-awareness and clarity; I needed to separate my own will from God's will.

Whenever you see me rubbing my hands together on the show, I am going through this internal process. I am asking myself the question: *Is this my will, or God's will?* If there is a tricky situation with a crew member it helps me take a beat and slow down my reaction to handle things the right way, with encouragement instead of anger.

On Season 2, when I had to discipline a crew member for crossing the line with a guest, I was pacing back and forth in the galley, wondering whether I'd been too hard on her. It was difficult for me to be tough on the crew knowing that, in the past, I'd done far worse. The footage never made it into the episode, but my producer Nadine was in fits of laughter in the control room as she saw me break the fourth wall and start talking to the camera. I was muddling through the right course of action like the Michael Scott character from *The Office*. To clear my head, I even dropped down to the floor and did a set of pushups. It was one of the tools from my toolkit in action.

The other tool, besides the deviation card, is a kind of checklist. Each time my brain is squirreling, or I feel upset, I take stock of the blocks and remind myself of the basic recovery steps. Did I eat right? Did I exercise? Did I do something kind or helpful for someone? Giving back gives me relief from that sense of hopelessness in mind and body. You must give back to hang on to the gift. Being selfless is selfish because it maintains my sobriety and keeps me pushing forward through the most challenging of situations.

The weather is beyond our control. So is loss, which will happen as long as we are alive. But, if I do my part and approach the wave with skill, I believe I will survive the storm. That doesn't mean I won't get slammed. I don't take the wave, because the wave could take me. It's far more powerful than I am. But I can approach the wave, paying close attention to its direction, height, and shifting currents.

FOLLOWING SEAS

There's another scene from the show that didn't make the cut. When we were filming Season 4 in France, I was trying to dock the boat in Monaco, but I found myself in what we captains call "following seas," stuck between the sea wall and a cruise ship the size of a city block. Following seas are rare. It's a type of sea that occurs behind a vessel, pushing it forward and at times lifting and slamming it down, in this case on top of what could have been the wall or the cruise ship. They are the most dangerous waters of all because they are so volatile and unpredictable, and they are virtually unnavigable.

In these situations, I commit to a course of action but make a backup or escape plan based on the worst that can happen. You stay committed to the approach and you follow through, but consider what you need for your option B. This time, I had two choices, either kill my crew if the boat slams against the sea wall, or possibly hurt a few people and damage both vessels if I hit the cruise ship port side. My approach factored in the latter possibility as I committed to a direction and continued to ride the waves, throttling up and down, turning my wheel over and over again to maintain some semblance of control. I was white-knuckling it, never letting go as I controlled my ascent on the rolls, which took us up two and three stories at a time. As all this was happening, a flotilla of tiny Laser sailboats decided to cross my path, like it was nothing.

"Oh my God, really? Really?! Seriously?" I exclaimed as my first officer and the film crew laughed at the absurdity of it all.

Thankfully, I made it without wrecking boats or killing anyone. Lesson learned: always call the harbormaster and learn the conditions inside the harbor before heading in.

While nowhere near as dramatic a situation, I found myself in "following seas" late in 2021 when I was giving a Power Point presentation to a room full of communications company CEOs at a global conference in Fort Lauderdale. There were 500 prominent executives in the audience, from AT&T, Comcast, and T-Mobile, among others. I was so proud of the slide show I had carefully prepared. It had little video clips embedded in some of the frames. One was from *Invictus*, the South African rugby movie I referenced in Chapter 8. The other was from that "Essence of Leadership" speech given by Colin Powell. It was powerful stuff, and the videos would have killed several minutes of my presentation time as they made my points for me.

But the technology failed. I had my pretty pictures, but I couldn't get the audio on the clips. *Oh my God, seriously?!*

So I ad-libbed. I didn't summarize the contents of the videos or paraphrase. Instead I used that very situation to highlight the fact that, no matter how well prepared you think you are, a wave will invariably come along and slam the side of your vessel.

"You see, this is what happens on a superyacht," I told them. "No matter how much technology is at our fingertips, something will fail us."

Of course, everyone laughed. But there was a more serious point to be made in the moment, so I continued:

"No matter how many times you replace a person with AI or some other digital tool, and no matter how much better you think it will be, some glitch will come along to mess you up. So you either need to be prepared to know how things function in that role, back to front, or retain the person who does. Humans who've been trained and have experience in a job are invaluable, so think twice about replacing a person with a thing!"

I can pivot in those situations because I know exactly what I want to say, and I've got my material down cold. Maybe you and your team spent months getting ready to roll out the international launch of a new, long-wearing, environmentally friendly brand of paint, but one of the markets has changed its regulations on how paint cans are labeled. But you've rehearsed this moment. Under your leadership, everyone in the supply chain has been laser-focused on getting this product out there. Your team knows exactly who to call in the procurement department to get that issue fixed stat, so that something that could have become a dealbreaker is no more than a glitch.

In these types of situations, where many things go wrong at once and I find myself in the middle of a figurative and literal maelstrom, my ADHD brain gives me the advantage. High pressure, deadlines, and certain kinds of chaos throw me into hyper focus and my squirrel brain disappears. What people think of as a weakness actually becomes my greatest strength. Maybe this is why I was born to be a captain.

There is growth and learning to be gained from all of life's following seas. Above all, they teach you to chart your course by looking inside yourself, then choosing a destination. Be bold enough to take the first step, flexible enough to alter your course according to life's circumstances, and persistent enough to muscle your way through.

Wrestling Through It

Tamyra Mensah-Stock, U.S. gold medalist wrestler in the 2021 Tokyo Olympics, made headlines with her spontaneous expressions of love for God and her country. Humble, grateful, and joyful, Tamyra won hearts as she did dozens of media interviews in the aftermath. But it was her description of how she prepared for her victory that really struck a chord with me. Tamyra described how she trained so hard, she felt she couldn't possibly endure another moment on the mat. Then her coach brought in one new wrestling opponent after another to take her down again and again. The lesson, of course, was perseverance and it was, in Tamyra's words, "brutal." Each kick and tumble was so painful she felt numb. But the training paid off, because when she was in the competition it was as if muscle memory took over, and something more.

"It's by the grace of God that I can even move my feet," she told an interviewer right after her winning match. "I just leave it in His hands."

Winning that gold was the hardest thing she'd done in her life, Tamyra shared. But she never doubted herself.

"I knew I could do it. I knew it would be hard. I prayed that I could do it. I kept going. I did it!"

I own my mistakes, admitting when I am wrong and learning from those moments. I am intentional about applying those early lessons from getting sober, and later life experiences, including the losses of family members. In those many moments of overwhelm, especially when I am on deck and surrounded by distraction, I take that extra beat to breathe. I remind myself that the rough waves will pass, but by staying true to myself and my higher purpose, I know I can weather any storm.

Even when that storm comes in the form of years of legal depositions. If you thought my Red Sea adventure was harrowing, having to deal with the insurance company lawyers after the fact was a doozy. Much worse than any pirate, they pulled out the stops to avoid having to pay a cent for what had happened in the Red Sea. Putting the blame entirely on me was their strategy.

The case had been tied up in the court system in the U.S. for five years when I got the call to fly back to Fort Lauderdale from Athens, where I'd been working. I had done my homework, documenting every moment of the ordeal; I could back up my statements with hundreds of photographs, so I knew I was on solid ground. But the process was still incredibly unnerving, which of course was their intention. The insurance company had spent five years to avoid spending at least $6 million in damages, half of which probably went toward legal fees.

I was summoned into a conference room where I was grilled for hours by a panel of 13 lawyers, all of them men. Each one had a go at me, attacking my judgment as a captain and questioning every decision I made. My friend John Allen, founder of Quantum Marine, which manufactured the hydraulic equipment for *White Star*, knew what had happened every step of the way but couldn't serve as a witness in the case because it was a conflict of interest. Instead, the company's attorney accused me of "failing to secure the boat."

"You're trying to blame me for your client's equipment failure when you should be thanking me that no lives were lost, and the vessel was saved," I shot back.

Another lawyer claimed we should never have left the anchorage in Yemen, and that the engine fire had happened because the vessel wasn't seaworthy. The boat was brand new!

"Let me remind you that we were anchored off a military camp in an unauthorized zone. We were lucky we weren't captured in the vessel, taken hostage, or killed. This is where you say, 'Thank you!' What's that I hear now? Crickets? Okay, I am done!"

And I walked out of the room in disgust.

I spent the next two weeks wondering if I would lose my captain's license. I didn't exactly crumple into a fetal position. But for too long there'd been a dark cloud of doubt hanging over my reputation, and it was infuriating. I should have been praised, not persecuted. Then finally a letter arrived, absolving me from all legal liability from the Red Sea incident.

The news was anticlimactic. I'd spoken my truth and stood my ground, then walked away with my head held high. I did all I had in my power to do. As far as I was concerned, the storm had passed, and I'd already proudly moved on.

- **Storms can blow up out of nowhere.** No matter how well you anticipate the weather. But those stormy moments can be both humbling and clarifying. They force you to make some hard choices, crystalizing what's most important in that life-and-death moment.

- **You can't control the storms, but you *can* ride them somehow.** My experiences at sea have taught me that setbacks and challenges, whether on water or land, dealing with death, illness, failure, or losses of any kind, are not necessarily within my control. I can't take that wave. But I can navigate my vessel to come out the other side with the least damage.

- **Some losses are a necessary wake-up call.** That series of unfortunate events may be God's way of putting you back on His path, which is the one you were meant to be on. Even the worst storms could be teaching you and positioning you for what's next.

- **Separate your will from God's.** Step back from the situation and think about whether your immediate goal or reaction is getting you to where you need to go. Let the waves roll but maintain your calm and approach them with skill.

- **You cannot do it alone.** Some losses are so great, like the death of a child, that it's hard to imagine a way out. People stay stuck. But with the help of others, and some powerful tools that we use in recovery, there is a way to get through to the other side. The storm will eventually clear, and you'll see the horizon.

Epilogue

PULLING INTO PORT

Never stop investing. Never stop improving.
Never stop doing something new.

—Bob Parsons, GoDaddy founder

People love to watch me squeeze into a slip, but not how you think! Over my 30-plus years in yachting, I've gained a reputation for smoothly easing 170-plus footers in and out of some of the tightest spaces in some of the busiest marinas in the world. I often draw a crowd as I pull in, with all eyes on me because people are shocked to see the size of the vessel, the alarmingly tight space, and the fact that a lady is at the helm.

There's a scene in Season 5 of *Below Deck Mediterranean* where I am docking in St. Tropez. It was a real squeaker. With huge yachts on either side of me and just inches between me and them, I really wished I had a rearview mirror. We were drawing quite the audience. People started videoing me on their phones, maybe because they were expecting me to knock into my neighbors, or they simply couldn't believe what they were seeing. Nadine in the production cabin next door was watching this play out on camera. Afterward she told me, "I was so stressed out watching you, I felt like I lost all bodily function." But I docked the vessel just fine.

What you didn't see, once the deckhands secured the ropes, was me walking off the vessel. There was an ice cream shop directly opposite us and it was all I could think about.

"I'm getting an ice cream," I announced. I deserved it!

I was able to pull off the ultimate docking feat because of how I'd trained my crew to communicate and move with careful agility, along with my own ability to multitask, all the while judging conditions and spaces down to the last millimeter. Docking that thing involves every one of my captaining skills coming together in that moment, elegantly demonstrating my three main pillars of discipline, integrity, and expertise. Once the fenders are out and the lines are tied, I take my crew out for dinner to show my gratitude and celebrate another job well done.

But the one thing I don't do are victory laps. I've won accolades and awards as a yacht captain. I get long messages full of love and admiration from fans of the show almost daily. I even have my own female impersonator, Ginger Snap, who stands in for me now and then on *Watch What Happens Live with Andy Cohen*. How cool is that? Yet none of this glory changes the fact that I must study and matriculate every year to keep up with my captain's license, or that every new charter location is like preparing for a college exam. Before each new journey I must study charts and read through stacks of thick books on local maritime conditions, like sea depths, safe anchorages, currents, weather patterns, as well as the local laws that determine where and when I can dock or drop anchor, or how close we can take boats and wave runners to the shore. The list of things to prepare for and familiarize myself with is endless.

Protecting and maintaining the reputation I have worked so hard to build in this industry is an ongoing process. As leaders, you already know that sustaining excellence requires constant effort, whether you find yourself at the end of a journey, halfway through, or at the start of a new one. And the learning must never stop. We live in an age of continual disruption, buffeted by new challenges both internally and externally, whether that's getting ahead of constantly evolving technology, dealing with economic uncertainty, or attracting and retaining new generations of talent with higher expectations of sustainability, accountability, work-life balance . . . you get the idea. So, none of us can afford to be complacent.

I am in constant forward motion, taking leadership to that next level, on dry land or at sea, and applying my principles of captaining to other arenas, including philanthropy, public speaking, entrepreneurship, and media. I've always got something new cooking. *The Ocean Rangers* animation series I am producing as I write this that teaches children about teamwork, recycling, ocean ecology, and marine safety is one project. I'm also starting a restaurant and launching a series of talks for business leaders. My restless squirrel brain is always on to the next challenge.

I mentioned before that I'm not one to look back. The past is the past, which is one of many reasons why I find those on-camera confessionals we do for the show so excruciating. Diving into my ancient history during the process of writing this book was tough, but at least it served a purpose: to share the many lessons I had to learn the hard way so that you, my reader, can use them to help you conquer your own future.

I've shared how my family and friends often tease that I've been given many lives. I know God spared me many times for a reason: to empower others to lead and become captains of their own lives. That next course is what I am charting for myself, and this journey is far from over!

INDEX

ACKNOWLEDGMENTS

To my sisters: Michelle, for always being the calm in the middle of my storms, and Kim and Sabrina, for loving me unconditionally through all those years of chaos.

To my dearest friends:

John and Fran Flynn, thank you for taking a chance on me, teaching me the foundations, and always wanting what was best for me.

John and Sharon Allen, for standing by my side during my darkest hour.

Randi Gold, no matter how much time passes I know you'll always be my sober sister. You're the one on my speed dial who picks up whatever the time of day or night.

Nadine Rajavi, my squirrel sister. Thank you for being kind with the edits. Above all, thank you for making *Below Deck Mediterranean* possible, fighting for me, and coming up with our code word, "Sweetpea."

Tania Hamidi, our conversations helped me stay centered. You have a gift.

To the Bravo executive team, thank for your support and for giving me the platform to be able to write this book.

To all the members of my crew, named and unnamed in this book, especially those who were with me long before the show. You taught me how to be a better listener, a better leader, and a better person.

To all the souls on board this book, identified or not, who allowed me to be a part of their lives and lent me their wisdom to share. And to the thousands of *Below Deck Mediterranean* fans who write to give me encouragement and tell their stories. I could not have continued to do this show without you.

To my editorial team:

My literary agent, Nicole Tourtelot, for guiding me through the book world and believing in my story. My editor, Melody Guy, and her team at Hay House. Thank you, Melody, for your kindness, grace, and patience. You showed up and were truly present for me. And my collaborator, Samantha Marshall, for hearing me, keeping my squirrel brain on course, and always bringing me back to "zero focus." I'm so glad I picked you!

Last, but not least, to all my nieces and nephews: Katie, TJ, and Jessie, and my great nieces and nephews, I love you all so much. And, Jeremy, my great nephew and adopted son, you had my heart from the moment I first laid eyes on you in that maternity ward. Though I may be the "fun" aunt to you guys, to me you are the children I never had, and you fill me with pride. If you learn only one thing from your Aunt Sandy, let it be this:

Always keep your eye on True North and navigate with grace through this life.

ABOUT THE AUTHOR

Captain Sandra Yawn, a.k.a. Captain Sandy, is a leader and businesswoman. As a renowned superyacht captain with over 30 years of international maritime experience, Captain Sandy has broken through the proverbial glass ceiling to achieve the highest status in an industry where women at the helm are rare. Not only has her integrity and courage earned her an outstanding reputation in an elite class of captain, she's earned accolades from the International Superyacht Society, which honored her with the prestigious Distinguished Crew Award. The distinction recognized Captain Sandy for her heroism in ensuring the safety of all guests, crew, and the vessel during a catastrophic fire in pirate-infested waters that occurred in 2006 off the coast of Yemen.

In 2015 when Captain Sandy became a series lead on Bravo's hit series *Below Deck Mediterranean*, she broke through yet another barrier to become a powerful female role model and one of the network's most beloved and respected personalities.

She is also a board member and benefactor for Captain Sandy's Charities and Visit Jacksonville. Additionally, Captain Sandy remains an active member of the Captain's Advisory Council for the Sea-Keepers Society, the International Superyacht Society, and the U.S. Superyacht Association.

Visit captainsandyyawn.com for more information.

Hay House Titles of Related Interest

THE SHIFT, the movie,
starring Dr. Wayne W. Dyer
(available as an online streaming video)
Learn more at www.hayhouse.com/the-shift-movie

***

*THE GAP AND THE GAIN: The High Achievers' Guide to Happiness,
Confidence, and Success,*
by Dan Sullivan, with Dr. Benjamin Hardy

THE HIGH 5 HABIT: Take Control of Your Life with One Simple Habit,
by Mel Robbins

HIGH PERFORMANCE HABITS: How Extraordinary People Become That Way,
by Brendon Burchard

*MARKET YOUR GENIUS: How to Generate New Leads, Get Dream Customers,
and Create a Loyal Community,* by Nikki Nash

*PASSION TO PURPOSE: A Seven-Step Journey to Shed Self-Doubt, Find
Inspiration, and Change Your Life,* by Amy McLaren

All of the above are available at www.hayhouse.co.uk.

CONNECT WITH

HAY HOUSE
ONLINE

🌐 hayhouse.co.uk   **f** @hayhouse

📷 @hayhouseuk   🐦 @hayhouseuk

▶️ @hayhouseuk   ♪ @hayhouseuk

'The gateways to wisdom and knowledge are always open.'

Louise Hay